FATHER TED

The Craggy Island Parish Magazines

Arthur Mathews & Graham Linehan

HAT TRICK

BOXTREE

First published in 1998 by Boxtree, an imprint of Macmillan Publishers Ltd,
25 Eccleston Place, London SW1W 9NF and Basingstoke

Associated companies throughout the world

ISBN 0 7522 2472 7

9 8 7 6 5 4 3 2 1

A CIP catalogue record for this book is available from the British Library

Picture credits

Associated Press/Topham: page 29
Nigel Davies: pages 1 *top right*; 6; 8; 14 *bottom*; 19 *bottom*; 20; 52 *bottom*
Mary Evans Picture Library: pages 31 *bottom*; 36 *top*; 60; 64
Scott Garrett: cover illustration and pages: 15 *top*; 16; 32; 36 *bottom right*; 42; 43; 50; 66; 67; 68; 76; 78; 79; 80
Hat Trick Productions Limited; pages 1 *top left*: 2; 6 *top left*; 7; 9 *top right*; 12 *bottom*; 14 *top*; 17; 36; 41; 44; 49 *top left*; 45; 54; 55; 57 *top left*; 62 *top left*; 77 *top left*; 85 *top right & bottom right*; 88
Hulton Getty: pages 1; 21; 22 *bottom*; 24 *top right*; 26; 28; 31 *top*; 35 *right*; 37; 40; 61; 74 *top right*; 77
Arthur Mathews: pages 34; 46 *top*; 56; 59 *top*; 75; 82
Guillaume Mustaars: 38 *top*; 51 *right*; 52 *top* and *centre*
Tony Stone pages 13 *top*; 22 *top*; 24 *bottom left*; 35 *bottom left*; 39; 46 *bottom left*; 63 *bottom right*
*Top*ham: pages 10; 15; 23; 24 *bottom left*; 25 *bottom left*; 32; 33 *bottom*; 38 *bottom*; 47; 49; 57 *bottom*; 59 *bottom left*; 62; 63 *top* and *bottom left*; 65 *bottom*; 70' 71 *top*; 73 *right*; 81; 83; 85 *bottom left*

Cover illustration: Scott Garrett with special thanks to Patrick and Cheryl McCormack of the Glan Quin House, Kilnaboy, County Clare

This book is a work of fiction. Names, characters, places, organizations, and incidents are either products of the authors' imagination or used fictitiously. Any resemblance to actual events, places, organizations, or persons, living or dead, is entirely coincidental.

Every effort has been made to contact all copyright holders. In case of error, please write to the publisher to ensure a full acknowledgement in future editions

Designed by Nigel Davies
Edited by Clare Hulton
Reproduction by Speedscan Ltd
Printed by Bath Press

CONTENTS

Dedicated to Frank Kelly, Pauline McLynn, Ardal O'Hanlon and especially to our dear friend Dermot Morgan

INTRODUCTION

Welcome to the introduction of this collection of Craggy Island Parish Magazines. I hope you will find much within these pages to entertain and inform.

I was reminded more than once during the many hours I spent compiling this collection of the fate of Father Leo Cleft, an old friend of mine from college days. Father Leo was sent to an outlying region of what was then the Belgian Congo, and one of his many innovations there was to start up a local parish magazine. It was not a successful venture, mostly because the natives could not read or understand the English language, and if they had, they would not have been interested in many of the self-penned articles, such as the history of the Gaelic Athletic Association in Tullamore. However, his folly was unexpectedly turned to his advantage after he offended a local tribal chief by telling an off-colour joke at a baptism. (Alas, he had made a visit or two too many visits to the punch bowl, and was not in full control of his faculties.) He thought it prudent to make a swift exit, and was able to cobble together a rudimentary paper raft from the unread newsletters. He escaped upriver where he sought refuge in a rubber plantation run by Father Pat Smyth from Navan.

But destiny had another cruel twist in store for him. At a christmas party, sadly drunk again, he fell into a vat of molten rubber. That was the end of Father Leo. It is rumoured that a section of his head was found in a tennis ball at an invitation tournament in Dublin, and it is a comforting thought that at least part of him eventually found his way home.

I hope such a fate does not befall me!

Seriously, I hope you enjoy these collected newsletters. I certainly had a 'grand time' going through them again, and I hope you will too.

Father Ted Crilly

OUR PARISH

Craggy Island, November 17, 1996

Many parishioners have remarked on my sermon at last Sunday's eight o'clock mass, when I talked about whether it's possible that hens know the difference between venial and mortal sins. Can a hen knowingly steal an egg from another hen, for example? Or is a hen capable of malicious damage? Unfortunately I heard gossip outside the church afterwards to the effect that I had run out of topics for sermons, and that I was making up the whole thing off the top of my head. Nothing could be further from the truth, as anyone who heard my sermon at Monday's evening mass will agree, when I gave what I thought was a well researched and persuasive talk on the subject of space travel.

It is disappointing when one spends up to twenty minutes preparing a sermon that one hears rumours to the effect that I am not taking the whole 'sermon thing' seriously. I would remind parishioners that to harbour such thoughts about a priest would carry a mandatory death sentence in the Middle Ages, and while I am sure that none of us would want to return to the days when you could be killed just for thinking about things, we can still learn a lot from the no-nonsense approach of the Church of the fifteenth century.

On a lighter note, it is my birthday next week, and a special collection will be made at all masses next Sunday for my holiday fund. I am planning to go to Cyprus this year (approximate cost: £450) so hopefully we can all make that extra special effort to send me off to the sun with a smile on my face.

I want to go here

Mass in the fourteenth century (lots of priests!)

100 GREAT PRIESTS

1. Father Noel Bells

Anyone who knew Noel Bells before his name was unfortunately dragged across the newspapers in the Summer of 1997 will know that there was more to him than being a paedophile priest. In most of the lengthy press reports of the time there was little mention of the lighter side of Noel's character — the man who loved horse racing, the nature lover who worshipped the great outdoors, the gentle soul who was never happier than when he was discussing the lyrics of the latest Spice Girls album with a group of young girls.

To those of us who thought we knew Noel well, the revelation that he was completely sex crazy came as a surprise, but when we thought back to those days we shared in St Colm's Seminary, we could recall certain tell-tale signs: the 'raunchy' magazines one would find blocking the chimney or hidden under a layer of ice at the bottom of the freezer; the jangling sound that accompanied him everywhere as he compulsively fiddled with the spare change in his pocket (indeed, this was how he earned his nickname 'Jingle Bells') and the way he would often say 'I'm very, very interested in sex' while raising his eyebrows suggestively and prodding you with his elbow. 'You know what I'm talking about,' he would continue.

The founder member of the short-lived St. Colm's Naturist Society, Noel's passion for running around in the nip was legendary. It was alleged that he once said a mass in the nude and accidentally summoned up demons. Such was his love of life, Noel would have laughed off the whole affair, and gone for a jog around the crease in the skimpiest pair of shorts ever seen in Christendom!

Now, Noel's confessional is a lonely prison cell, to which there is no key (except the one that lets him out for exercise) and although twenty years seems like a long time, his renowned gifts for conjuring up sexual fantasies will almost certainly make time pass quickly.

2. Father Billy Roundtree

'Come see the chapel at Mullinahinch,
'tis the talk of all the county,
with mighty windows of stained glass,
and all of Billy Roundtree.'

Such was the fame of Father Billy Roundtree in the early fifties that schoolchildren around his parish of Mullinahinch in Offaly used to sing the above ballad on their way home from school. A very, very ugly man (so ugly, in fact, that it was said that wind would go around him rather than risk touching his face), Father Roundtree was nevertheless a vain man. What else could

the tastefulness of this
image. Did it not show
Father Roundtree as
equal, if not superior
to, God Himself? Father
Billy responded to
criticism by ignoring
it. That was his way.

Similarly, his
parochial house was not
filled with statues of
Our Lord or holy
pictures, but with
massive posters and
plaster-cast models
depicting himself as a
saint or a 'Hawaii Five-
O' type policeman. In
many ways, God was again
seen in a subservient
role.

The old man died at
the age of seventy-six
in 1980. The State
funeral he had requested
in his will, attended by
Heads of State, Royalty
and film stars never
materialised. This, no
doubt, would have
displeased him
immensely. But the
chapel at Mullinahinch
still stands, and to this
day a visitor can enjoy
the stained-glass Father
Billys — a reminder of
an extraordinary man.

Father Roundtree

explain his decision to portray himself
in the stained glass windows of his
church at Mullinahinch? There he could be
seen striking various heroic poses such
as wrestling lions and slaying dragons,
dressed only in a loincloth. The main
window behind the altar showed him
entering Heaven as various angels and God
himself bowed before him. Many questioned

WHEN DINOSAURS RULED CRAGGY ISLAND

by Father Ted Crilly

Big monsters, the size of houses, destroying everything in their path. Stomping about all over the place and feared by all the other creatures of the planet. No, I'm not talking about tax inspectors!!! I'm talking about dinosaurs, those fearsome beasts that terrorised the world for literally zillions of years before time began. It's hard to imagine our own lovely Craggy Island being home to those oversized grotesque lizards, but that was almost certainly the case. Of course, they didn't live in houses, but in nests made out of giant twigs. Twigs then, of course, would have been generally bigger than they are now, as were most things. Grass would generally have been much longer as well, and not just because there weren't any lawnmowers!!! It was just generally longer.

The people who inhabited Craggy Island at the time of the monsters would have worn very few clothes. The men would have gone around in loincloths made out of tiger skins, and would have carried clubs and things like that. The women would have worn bras made out of tiger skins and furry hats in the winter made from rabbits. Of course lipstick and perfume would not have existed at the time, so the women would not spend endless hours looking in mirrors (also non-existent at the time) making themselves up. (How different from the ladies of today!) As electric razors, and even non-electric razors, had yet to be invented, men would have had big beards and communicated with each other using grunts and very simple words. It was also common to see the husbands dragging some of the more unruly wives round by the hair! (What would some of today's 'women's libbers' have to say about that!)

Because Craggy Island was so small, there would only have been room for about eleven dinosaurs on the island. These would have included the deadly raptors, who hunted in packs and had the ability to turn door handles, the mighty Tyrannosaur, who could not see you if you stood still because it had wonky chicken eyes, the Petrodactus, which was able to fly and had a terrifying 'Caw! Caw!' cry, and the dinosaur with the horns.

The people of this time would have had battles with the monsters, and often men with blonde hair would have battles with men with black hair. Thus, it was a violent time, with no place for cissies. But then a man with black hair would fall in love with a woman with blonde hair, and they would go off and do 'you know what', leading eventually to modern civilisation.

Of course, all this was a long time ago, but have people really changed that much? Well, today we don't live in caves and live in constant fear of giant monsters, so the answer would have to be yes.

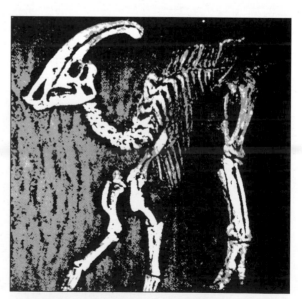

Actual proof that dinosaurs were on Craggy Island. This skeleton can be seen in the wall of Mrs Quinn's parlour.

c Father Ted Crilly

In the 1980s a complete dinosaur skeleton from the island was used in a travelling puppet show. It needed eight puppeteers to operate it.

HOUSEHOLD TIPS FOR LADIES, WIVES AND MOTHERS with MRS DOYLE

1. Making a bed

PREPARATION

Always enter the bedroom well groomed and confident of doing a good job. I find that if I am depressed when I am about to make a bed, my work will suffer and the bed will look crumpled and strange after I have finished with it. Always make sure that there is no one in the bed before you begin. (An obvious tip, but you'd be amazed at the amount of times this happens!)

EARLY STAGES: THE APPROACH TO THE BED, THE UNDERSHEET AND MATTRESS

Always approach the bed from a westerly position. Do not rush up to the bed, but move towards it slowly. Sometimes a bed can sense that the person about to make it has no real plan, and this can lead to a loss of confidence on the bed maker's part when it comes to the later stages of shaking the pillows and arranging the eiderdown.

On arriving at the side of the bed, grab the blankets and sheets firmly, and pull across the main body of the bed until all are in a neat bundle at the bottom of the mattress. You may feel tired at this stage, but that is a normal feeling and there is no need to feel pessimistic about your ability to complete the task. Next, remove the undersheet and disinfect the main body

of the mattress if necessary. If you find a hot water bottle, remove it and place to the side of the room.

THE TOP SHEET AND LOWER BLANKET

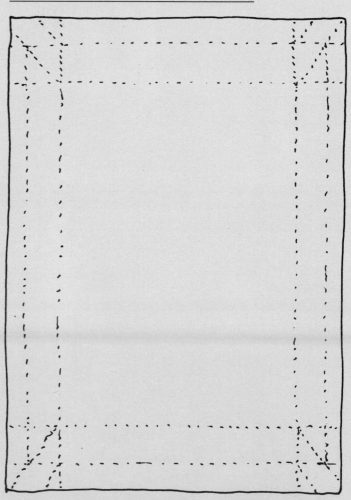

It may help to mark the fold lines on your sheets before starting to make the bed.

Many ladies become panicky and anxious when they have to deal with the top sheet. 'Will I do a good top sheet job?' is a question that comes up time and time again in ladies' conversations. But it is really a very straightforward procedure. The sheet is merely laid across the bed, horizontally and vertically, until the width and breadth of the bed is adequately covered. The sheet is then straightened out, and any air bubbles trapped underneath can be removed by beating with a stick or wooden club. 'I see a crease!' many ladies scream at this stage, but creases are not unusual in bed making, and can be easily eradicated. Firm pulling of the sheet at both sides (you may need another lady to help you with this) usually solves this problem.

The lower blanket is then laid over the top sheet. There is a tendency at this stage amongst many ladies, especially younger ones, to lapse into over-confidence; we've all come across this moment - 'Oh, I've done the difficult bit, this is very straightforward, there won't be a problem.' Danger! This is when a slothful or sluggish attitude can set in, and result in the most terrible of consequences: 'the ragged bed'. The maker of a 'ragged bed' is of no use to herself or her husband and may as well go and live on a rock somewhere. A 'ragged bed' maker can often turn into an alcoholic lady and abandon her family for the cheap thrill of a half bottle of sherry. So, I stress again, it is very important to do a good 'lower blanket job'.

The final stage, at least during the summer months (extra top blankets may be needed during chilly winter months), is the laying of the eiderdown. In Hindu countries this is a solemn moment indeed, and it is not unusual for the Hindi lady to be joined by her entire family to witness the occasion accompanied by a local 'guru' or 'holy man' who may chant mournfully during the proceedings. However, I personally would find that a distraction, although many

ladies like to listen to light-headed music playing on the radio during this part of the bed making.

The eiderdown is applied very much like the lower blanket. However, unlike the lower blanket, it is never tucked in. Consequences of tucking the eiderdown in include: risk of infection, blanket spillage, 'hard shoulder' and lice. Thankfully, it is a rare occurrence, and is both unnecessary and ugly.

The 'bad bed'.

LOOKING AT YOUR BED AFTER YOU'VE FINISHED MAKING IT

Always have a good look at the bed after you've made it. Watch out for creases, grease marks and signs of over-enthusiasm (the double fold on the lower sheet may have seemed like a good idea at the time, but does it help the overall 'atmosphere' of the bed?). If you feel like it, there is nothing to stop you leaving a cherry or small flower on the bed as a final touch, but this can be misunderstood by the bed dweller as either a sign of over familiarity or out and out madness. In bed making, as in life, 'less is more'.

HAPPY BED MAKING!

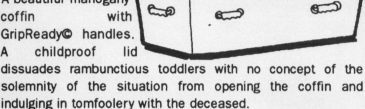

Notices.

An incident referred to in last week's parish bulletin involving <u>Father Jack Hackett</u> and a <u>young holidaymaker from Sweden</u> has been resolved happily to everybody's satisfaction. However, to persuade the young lady against taking legal action, the sum of £500 had to be diverted from parish funds. This money was originally intended as prize money for our annual 'All-Priests' sports day, so I am afraid a special charge will have to be made for anyone who wishes to avail themselves of confession from next Monday on. Also, instead of handing out a long, and frankly, rather boring string of prayers to say, I will accept money as penance instead. I am afraid I am as yet unable to accept payment by credit card.

<u>Father Dougal McGuire</u> has lost a <u>skipping rope</u>. The rope, approximately ten feet in length, has wooden handles with 'I love The Beatles' written in marker on one handle. There is no reward for its return, since as it belongs to a priest, it is your moral duty to give it back if you find it.

OUR PARISH

Craggy Island, December 22, 1996

This week is a landmark issue for 'Our Parish' as we bring you our first 'colour' edition. I well remember seeing my first colour film, the original version of 'The Fly' with Vincent Price, and I'm sure that this edition of your new look newsletter will have the same effect on you as that had on me. Some of you may remember a previous colour edition of the magazine, which was hand done by Father McGuire using crayons. While this was very popular, it took Father McGuire a full week, and that was simply to colour in a duck in yellow for an article about farmyard animals. This time, however, the magazine

has been professionally coloured by the printers, and we're confident that the result will be pleasing. Of course that does not mean that other areas of 'Our Parish' will suffer either in terms of quality or quantity. An attractive mixture of amusing, informative and not overly serious (excluding religious ethical stuff) articles is what we aim for, and we have no plans to change this tried and tested 'winning formula.'

Christmas is nearly upon us once again. Many people ask me why it is that Easter moves around a bit in the calendar, while Christmas is always on December 25. That's a good question. However, it is a question I have no answer for. It may possibly be something to do with the weather or the type of heating that they had in Israel at the time Our Lord lived there. I don't know. Why he chose to be born at such a cold time of the year is His business. The whole thing about Catholicism is best summed up in the phrase 'you can lump it or leave it'. You don't have to believe any of it, but if you do, then the best thing is just to go along with it and not think about it too much. Our hospitals are only too full of people who thought about religion a little bit more than they should have.

But back to the true meaning of Christmas. It is traditional at Christmas Day Mass to read out the 'Christmas dues', that is, the amount of money that individual parishioners donate to the Church at this very special feast. It gave me no pleasure at all last year to disclose the fact that BENNY COOGAN donated a mere £3. Benny clearly forgot that I had dragged myself away from watching the Galway races on television earlier that year to officiate at his daughter's wedding. Hopefully he will be slightly more generous this Christmas. Our parish motto this year should be 'Don't be like Benny, spend more than a penny.'

CRAGGY ISLAND CHRISTMAS DUES	
Dan Smiley	£100 (!)
Vance Collins	£50
Colm Topol	£50
Eddie Hedges	£100 (!)
Mrs Cullen	£2
Mrs Fancy Allen	£5
Mrs O'Neill	£7
Frank Munaghan	£25
Fergus Verdon	£12
Mrs Skillet	£6
Mrs O'Mann	£90
Mrs Sullivan	£20
Mrs Hangaran	£6
Eugene Tait	£10

Christmas is nearly upon us once again. Many people ask me why it is that Easter moves around a bit in the calendar, while Christmas is always on December 25. That's a good question. However, it is a question I have no answer for. It may possibly be something to do with the weather or the type of heating that they had in Israel at the time Our Lord lived there. I don't know. Why he chose to be born at such a cold time of the year is His business. The whole thing about Catholicism is best summed up in the phrase 'you can lump it or leave it'. You don't have to believe any of it, but if you do, then the best thing is just to go along with it and not think about it too much. Our hospitals are only too full of people

100 GREAT PRIESTS

3. *Father Hercules Staunton*

Father Hercules Staunton outdoors in Canada

'I'll tell you something about the Great Outdoors,' said Father Hercules Staunton to his congregation at Castlederg in the early '60's. 'It's great. And it's outdoors.'

This single line echoes through the years as an example of what Father Staunton became famous for: his love of nature and his constant struggle to make his sermons interesting. He was not a natural orator, and his congregation would sometimes faint at the monotony of his sermons. 'They were the lucky ones,' says his curate of the time, Father Pierce Breezly. As they left Mass, one often noticed the pale skin of the members of his flock, the deadness of their eyes, the lumpen movements of their limbs as they made their way home. Even then, the exhilaration of leaving his tiny church at Castlederg at the end of Mass on Sundays could not counter the realization that next Sunday they would have to come back and listen to Father Staunton all over again.

What was his greatest sermon? There are many contenders. The time he likened matrimony to manure? His A to Z of sin, where he spent twenty minutes trying to think of a vice beginning with the letter D? His comparison of the Last Supper to the 1960 Grand National? All have their supporters. But is it proper even to try and select one? All his sermons were dull, all his arguments muddled and confused, his every word delivered in a low whine, often with a gap of several minutes between sentences.

Joe MacNeill, an unremarkable man from the nearby town of Newfergus, was the man who ended Father Staunton's life in January 1964. During a lecture on the meaning of Lent one grey Sunday morning Joe leapt to the pulpit and delivered a mortal blow to the old man with a candlestick which had been placed on the altar. He was the first of Father Staunton's parishioners to crack, and although few would have supported the extreme violence he used to terminate the flow of the cleric's meanderings, many, secretly in their hearts, applauded what he had done. The monotony, at last, was over.

THE HISTORY OF CRAGGY ISLAND

1690-1750

'Oh, Craggy Isle,
wondrous rock cast upon the sea,
come gale, come storm,
and lash our lovely rock!'

The powerful verse above comes from McConville's History of Ireland's Islands, first published in Cork in 1885, and was written by Pierce Conmey, the one-legged bandit/poet from Tuam who lived on Craggy Island for some weeks early in 1697, before chronic depression and alcoholism drove him back to the mainland.

It is the first recorded mention of the island in literature, although it is almost certain that it existed for many years beforehand. In fact, many theories suggest that it is one of Ireland's oldest islands, probably dating back to early geographical times. In those days, like now, it consisted mostly of rock, grass, and small stretches of unusual brown sand. A census carried out in 1690 recorded that there were five inhabitants

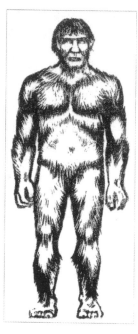

Two artist's impressions of Peter McGroom, who became governor of Canada

The field at Dunfin that used to be the site of a stone age fort.

During the great storm of 1720, waves this big managed to submerge the island completely

of the island - 'Two men, two women and an animal-like creature whose sex is indeterminable'. (This was almost certainly Peter McGroom, who many years later became governor of Canada.) The census also mentioned that 'the typical Craggy Islander is light of heart and head, terrified of fire, and prone to fits of debilitating anxiety'.

By 1695 the island was officially

This cliff used to be four feet to the left, before 'The Big Wind' of 1733.

upgraded from a rock to an island, and a charter to this effect can be found in the library of Trinity College, Dublin. The legendary stone age fort at Dunfin, at the north of the island, was knocked down around this time to make way for a field. Across the field was a shop, selling household goods and cheese.

*   *   *   *   *

During the period from 1700 to 1719, gales lashed the island incessantly, and people often tied themselves to posts to prevent themselves from being blown into the sea. 1720 saw the worst storm in the history of the world, and Craggy Island was right at the receiving end, being entirely submerged for two weeks. Twenty people were drowned, and several floated away, some as far as Gibraltar. Survivors who stayed on the island were forced to stand on tippy toes for the duration, barely managing to keep their mouths and noses above water. Among them was Father Xavier Smith, who kept up spirits by

The site of The Battle of the Big Hedge.

knocking down every house over two feet tall. Sheep and pigs who had not been nailed down were swept over cliffs, and trees, and even large patches of grass, were pulled from their roots by the sheer ferocity of the gales.

*   *   *   *   *

The decade 1740 to 1750 beome known in latter years as 'the troubled decade'. A fierce civil war broke out on the island between the Haves, who owned the turf on the island, and the Have Nots, an illiterate mob of vagabonds and ruffians. Skirmishes erupted at various intervals during this time, the worst atrocities occurring at the Battle Of The Big Hedge in 1748, when a kicking match broke out between a group of Haves and some Have Nots. This infamous conflagration, after a Have dance where the Have Nots were refused admission, resulted in a bruised shoulder for the Have Not leader, Tommy Vants, who soon afterwards left the island for America, where he became a successful travel agent. Finally, in January 1750, the Bishop of Galway, Dr Walt Stone, issued a proclamation declaring that kicking people in the head was 'a grave sin', and peace was restored. Dr Stone himself was a native of 'Craggy', and was the first man from the island to wear aftershave.

shocking the islanders with bawdy tales from his time as a parish priest in San Francisco. At one stage he was told to 'Eff off' by one of the islanders, who had climbed to the top of a tree to escape the rising tide, such were the offensive and sexist nature of his stories.

1733 will always be remembered for 'The Big Wind', and was also famous as the year when the sun failed to shine even once. Dense clouds covered the island for eleven months out of twelve, and it was often so dark that days were indistinguishable from nights. In August, gales of three hundred miles an hour succeeded in blowing the island four miles further away from the mainland and

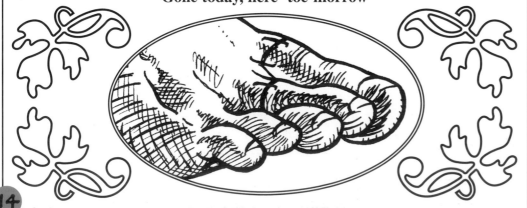

CRAGGY ISLANDERS ABROAD

It's always good to hear news of Craggy Island natives doing well in a distant country, so when we heard that John Cloney had been appointed hangman at Bangkok's world-famous Hinkwin prison, we were very pleased indeed. John left the Island in 1965, and worked for many years as an informer for the dreaded Stasi security police in Romania until threats forced him to leave the country. He then became a torturer for the much feared General Ricardo-Alfonz Pizzi in Colombia, where he worked alongside another Craggy Islander, Eugene Mullen, using violence and intimidation to secure information from the rebels opposed to the military regime. His methods were vicious in the extreme, but amongst those who suffered at his hands, very few did not respect John and appreciate the tenacity and good humour with which he approached his grisly task. We wish him well in his new position.

Eileen Dineen has died in Australia after being bitten by a rabid kangaroo. The beast, who chased Eileen for several miles before delivering the fatal bite, was later shot dead by police marksmen. Eileen

left Craggy Island in the early sixties and worked on the Apollo Space Programme for several years, where she had responsibility for the astronauts' cutlery and plates.

Denis Knowles has died in New Zealand after an experiment in Wellington University went tragically wrong. Denis, who had been working on a top-secret project to make monkeys bigger, was stomped to death by a Borneo tree monkey after he let it roam free in the laboratory unsupervised for several days. The monkey, called Seamus, grew to over twelve feet tall and stomped Denis to death after he had returned from an all-night drinking session in a local pub to celebrate Ireland's latest Eurovision Song Contest success.

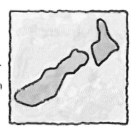

Seamus shortly after killing Denis

Notice
Winners of the International Personality of the Year as voted by parishioners at last Sunday's masses: 1. Sean Connery 2. Madonna 3. Nelson Mandela and Hugh Grant (joint third). None of the winners will be attending the awards ceremony in the Doanmore Hotel on January 5th.

JUST FOR FUN!

* <u>Note to Parents</u> — Jokes with a slightly 'blue' content have been marked with an asterix.

** <u>Note to general readers</u> — Jokes with a double asterix indicate that the joke may be recounted here incorrectly, either because a crucial turn of phrase or pun was misheard when the joke was recounted to the editors, or because the joke was recounted incorrectly to the editors in the first place. The editors take no responsibility for jokes that fail to induce the proper response.

<u>An Innocent Mistake</u>
(conts: 'Cheeky Talk')

** A priest was taking a catechism class in a school one day. 'Who made the world?' he asked one small boy. 'I don't know,' said the boy, 'but he must have had a big appetite.' The priest was confused until he realised that the boy had misheard him and thought he had said 'ate the world' instead of 'made the world.'

<u>Double Meaning Habit Mistake</u>
(conts: 'Nun "having a laugh with a Priest")

     Priest to Nun: 'I thought you'd given up smoking, Sister Imelda?'

     Nun to Priest: 'No, Father. I'm afraid I can't break the habit!'

<u>It's Not a Miracle</u>
(conts: 'Naked Priest')

* Two priests, Father Pat and Father Sean, went to Lourdes. Father Sean had had back pains for years and was hoping for a miracle cure. He changed into his swimming trunks and went for a dip in the holy waters. Things took a turn for the worse, however, when the elastic on his trunks snapped, and he realised that he was in the nude. He called for help to Father Pat, who was waiting for him at the side. 'Help me, Father Pat! Could you get me a towel?'

     While Father Pat went looking for a shop, a nun that he knew passed by.

     'Ah, Father Sean,' she said. 'You must be here because of the pain in your back. Are you looking for a miracle?'

     'No', said Father Pat. 'Just a pair of swimming trunks!'

<u>Who Confusion</u>
(conts: 'Rock Music')

     Young Trendy Priest to Old 'Fuddy Duddy' Priest: 'Have you heard the new album by The Who?'

     'What?'

     'No! The Who!'

Notices.

The answers to last week's 'Our Parish' Quiz were -
1: Jessica Lange. 2: An elephant's is larger. 3: Roddy Doyle, and 4: 'You can do that if you want, but it'll take you a year to get the splinters out of your arse.'
The quiz was sponsored by Reilly's Garage 'Where Cars Are Cheaper Than Vans'.

OUR PARISH

Craggy Island, January 19, 1997

You may notice a few differences with this week's 'Our Parish.' The use of an 'Apple Mac' computer has led to a fresh design initiative and loosed us from the chains of sticking down bits of copy (that's 'type' to You, The Layman!) with glue.

While there are bound to bee hiccups when @ @ @ @ @ @, we are sure to get the hang of it very soon, and I can safely guarantee that as we geett to grripps with the new technological set-up, future 'Our Parishes' will be bigger and brighter.

I am always open to ideas from parishioners on how to improve our little publication, and a suggestion that I have heard more than once is to 'have less religion in it'. This is exactly the kind of thing that Stalin would have said during the early days of Communism, and I'm afraid it's a big 'no-no' as far as I'm concerned. Religion is a very important part of Catholicism, and will continue to play a prominent role in your 'new-look' parish newsletter, even in the post-religious world.

'WHY ARE PRIESTS SO HOLY?'

That is a question I have heard more than once during my many years 'wearing the cloth'. Well, as the American entertainer Al Johnson once said, 'You either have it or you don't', and I think when it comes to being holy, priests certainly 'have it'. As a priest, do I feel holier than my parishioners? That is another difficult question. No doubt every parishioner feels different levels of holiness. Some, in fact, probably feel not very holy at all. They are the 'bad people'. The ones who 'spoil it for everybody else'. We all know somebody like that. It

This picture of me doing one of my sermons was kindly taken by Mrs O'Keefe. It's a shame it wasn't taken by her son Eugene, who sits three places to her right.

The halometer chart showing holiness levels: John Woods, Most People, Father Jimmy Bifton, Father Dougal, Me, Mother Theresa. The Halometer scale: VERY HOLY, QUITE HOLY, HOLYISH, NOT VERY HOLY, NOT AT ALL HOLY.

may be improper to single out one individual at this point, but I have never liked JOHN WOODS, who is an electrician from Sligo. He overcharged me for doing a shoddy repair job on a television once, and that has always annoyed me.

Anyway, let us now address the question of what it means to be 'unholy'. What can you say about people who are a bit on the unholy side? I think we all know someone who has a 'vibe' of unholiness about him. Anybody who steals a bike, for example, would automatically put himself in an unholy state. To put it another way, lets us look at a 'graph of holiness'. If the graph starts at 0, indicating a complete lack of holiness, and climbs to 100, which would indicate a state of complete holiness, it would be fair to say that priests would inhabit the bit going from 75 to 100, while lay people would tend to congregate around the 25 mark. That would be a general rule, however, and not an absolute one. Mother Teresa of Calcutta, for instance, would be holier than Father Jim Bifton, who ran a vice ring in Galway for many years.

The whole 'holiness' thing is an interesting topic, and one I shall no doubt return to in the future.

HOUSEHOLD TIPS FOR LADIES, WIVES AND MOTHERS with MRS DOYLE

2. Doing a salad

THE WHOLE SALAD 'THING'

A few years ago, the 'salad dish' was almost unknown in Ireland. Certainly, things like tomatoes and beetroot were grown in fields and gardens, but only to be put in sandwiches or eaten on their own, like apples. Anybody who would have seriously proposed that a pile of carrots and vegetables on a plate would be a meal in itself would have been taken out and shot. Of course, men especially, but ladies as well, will always prefer a decent 'real meal' of meat, potatoes and boiled vegetables to a salad dish, but if guests pop by unexpectedly, then a simple salad, whether they want one or not, is a great way to pass the time with them.

PREPARATION

Be careful about what type of vegetables you want to put into your salad. It would be easy just to stick a big turnip or a pile of onions on a plate and leave it like that, but any lady who does such a thing is making a grave mistake. It is better to get a few 'gentler' vegetables such as a tomato or lettuce and arrange them in a pleasing combination on the plate, which should be daintily sized and have a pretty flower pattern.

SLICING THE VEGETABLES

Always slice the vegetables into small pieces, rather than throwing them on to the plate in a haphazard form. Use a knife rather than a broken bottle. The jagged edge of a broken bottle is certainly sharp, but shards of glass can often stick in the vegetables, causing horrendous intestinal and facial injuries to your guests. No, it is better to use a knife.

Place the vegetable on the table rather than holding it in your other hand while slicing, and use a downward 'chopping' action with your knife. Remember: the sharper the knife, the less time it will take to go through the vegetable, and the more time you will have for other household activities.

PUTTING THE SLICED VEGETABLES ON THE PLATE.

Wrong.

Right.

Put the sliced vegetables on the plate. Then place a little bit of salad cream or mayonnaise on the edge of the plate closest to your guest. If the salad cream is placed on the edge of the plate furthest away from your guest, he may accidentally dip the cuffs of his shirt into the vegetables on his 'way across', and then swear at you. Avoid this situation at all costs.

TIDYING UP AFTERWARDS

Never force your guests to eat every bit of vegetable on the plate. There are always 'left-overs' after every meal, and these can nearly always be fed to dogs. Washing plates is usually easier after a meal of salads, and sometimes plates don't have to be washed at all. (A joyous moment for every lady!) The washing-up procedure is otherwise no different from any other kind of non-salad meal, but care and efficiency, as always, are recommended. There is nothing worse than a slovenly lady who doesn't give a toss, and who prefers to spend her days in an alcoholic haze as her household goes to rack and ruin around her.

You can't tell that this plate has been used for a salad …

… but this plate after beef stew will need a lot of scrubbing!

THE HISTORY OF CRAGGY ISLAND

1777-1860

1777 saw the opening of the Aborigine prison on Craggy Island. Just as Irish convicts were banished to Tasmania, bad Aborigines were exiled to Craggy Island. The first shipment arrived in February of that year, and consisted mostly of 'white-collar' criminals such as those responsible for tax fraud or insider trading. The first murderers arrived in November, and were followed in December by animal rights activists, forgers and lesbians. The lesbians became immediately unpopular with the islanders when they opened a nudist beach but refused admission to local people. Murty Quiglan, an islander of the time, noted in his diary:

'The lesbians have barred native islanders from the nudist beach, as they suspect that the men will only go there to look at their jugs. However, the men of the island would be better employed staying at home and admiring the jugs on their own wives.'

The remnants of the original aboriginal lesbian nudist beach can still be seen on the northern shore of the island.

During the following decades, the Aborigines became assimilated into the local population, mostly due to the efforts of Steve Giggaging, who sired three hundred children between 1785 and 1840. These 'Cragoriginals', as they became known, embraced Craggy Island customs such as 'horse leaping' (jumping over horses from a standing position) and 'stick magic' (rolling sticks down hills). Over three thousand people from the mainland attended a stick magic event on the island in 1786, where the crowd were entertained by musical bands and alternative comedians of the day, including Johnny Bones, who offended pro-British spectators in the crowd with his hard-hitting material about English atrocities in the Far East.

Bad Aborigines (look at the state of them!)

Dancing Aborigines

*　　*　　*　　*　　*

Clinical depression is no stranger to the Craggy Islander, and, in fact, it is believed that islanders in general are predisposed to this unfortunate illness. 1802 was the year of the Great Depression on the island, when listlessness and a general lackadaisical attitude affected almost everybody, leading to the loss of over three thousand working days. Alcoholism is also a terrible curse that has affected the islanders over the years. The great census of 1805 showed that everybody on the island was a complete alcoholic, and also that 'binge drinking' was particularly rampant. Bulimia, anorexia nervosa and other eating and drinking disorders were also prevalent in the early nineteenth century, affecting everybody from babies to men in their eighties. In fact, it was not unheard of for an islander to suffer from up to 130 eating and drinking disorders at the same time. But despite all this, the locals were mercifully free from drug abuse until the early 1850s, when a shady character arrived on the island selling hash and an early version of E. This was 'Disreputable' Dan O'Neill, who had served several years in Indian jails for drug offences. Setting himself up as a music promoter and entrepreneur, his real reason for coming to the island was to lure the local young people, most of whom were adjusting to normal life again after the ravages of the Great Famine, into a life of drug dependency and cocaine addiction. Weakened by the years of hunger, they soon succumbed to his tales of how 'cool' it was to take drugs and be out of your head all the time. His job done, and after having made several pounds, a fortune in those days, O'Neill headed off to Edinburgh, where he lured several members of the Royal family into amphetamine abuse.

*　　*　　*　　*　　*

How did these people fit into this small house?

One of the great characters of Craggy Island during the middle of the nineteenth century was Seamus O'Groinne, a famed storyteller or *seanachi* (literally, someone who tells stories, or vice versa). 'Old Seamus' as he was always known, even as a young man, had a collection of over twenty million stories which he would tell round the fire to anyone who came to visit him in his cottage on the eastern shore of the island. Among these tales were 'An Fearr Mhath Bhic An Ceann' ('The Good Man With The Head') and 'Crann Seo Bhan Tigh Bhuic An Ceo' ('The Shepherd's Pie'). Many of his stories were written down and recorded for posterity by Sir Frederick Davies, a local landowner's son, who later became well known in the Irish literary revival of the late nineteenth century, and had his play 'The Green Pot' performed at

A scene from 'A'n Thu Mar Sin Amghaill'

the Abbey Theatre in 1905. He was hugely influenced by O'Groinne's stories, especially 'A'n Thu Mar Sin Amghaill' ('The Hairy Chin') about a girl who is captured by fairies and forced to think up plot lines for pornographic novels. Unwilling to write porn for fairies, she hides in a hedge for fifteen years until a posse of elves capture her and turn her into a couple of blades of grass. She is blown about by the wind for another twenty years, until a handsome prince comes along and mows the lawn, thus releasing her from her grass form and turning her back into a beautiful girl. However, when she kisses him, she finds out that he has a hairy chin and commits suicide. Sir Frederick wrote a play with music based on this story, but it was never performed in public.

100 Great Priests

⊱┈◈┈○┈◈┈⊰

4. Father Dinny Marbles

Whenever the name of Father Marbles is mentioned, the word 'hard' is never far away. 'He was a memorable character, all right,' says an old student of his, Father Herbert 'Guitar' Smith, who studied under the legendary man at St Colm's Seminary in the 1940s. Father Marbles had been a stalwart at St Colm's since the '20s, where as housemaster, he had gained the reputation as a 'tough old bird'. Rising at 4.30 every morning, he would say three masses in a row before setting forth on his rounds around the college. 'I'm off to wake up the boys,' he would say, as he set forth at great speed around the dormitories jangling his keys and hollering like a Confederate soldier from the American Civil War. 'We would hear him coming from a

distance of several hundred yards away,' says Father Smith. 'If you weren't out of bed by the time he arrived, he would climb in between the sheets with you and jab a key repeatedly into the small of your back. When you had got up he would then kick you to the ground and hop up and down on you for half an hour. If you as much as yelped he would stamp on your head in his big boots. All the time he would be singing his beloved Irish Republican songs. He was fiercely nationalistic as well.'

Father Marbles was also games master at St Colm's. He developed a special 'heavy ball' with protruding nails for the boys to play Gaelic football with. He also 'adapted' the game of hurling in the college to special 'St Colm's Rules' so that the boys were free to hit each other over the head with their hurling sticks. Another of his innovations allowed him, while acting as referee, to have his own stick and implement the rules by whacking boys who committed fouls. 'I should have some fun too, you know, lads!' he used to cry, as he charged around the playing field, administering rough justice to rule breakers.

His love of Latin was legendary. He had taught the subject in St Tadgh's Boarding School in Limerick before St Colm's, and his standards were exceptionally high. He expected his twelve-year-old students to be completely fluent in the language even before they'd had their first lesson, and anyone who could not hold a twelve-hour conversation with him about the second Roman invasion of Gaul after three lessons was routinely beaten.

There are not many like Father Marbles now. Some people would say that we have gone 'soft'. That the harsh discipline imposed by priests and teachers like Father Marbles did his students very little harm. They may indeed be right. The 'tough old bird' passed away in 1966. Perhaps it is just as well he never lived to see the age of Bob Geldof and satellite television. He would not have liked such things.

Father Marbles on a see saw

PORTRAIT of a PARISHIONER

Imelda Dowd

'My name is Imelda Dowd, and I am 100 years old exactly. I am still very active and live at home with a dog. Last year I was blown up in an explosion when I plugged a set of Subbuteo floodlights into the mains. I spent three months in hospital, and during that time I met Bob Geldof.

I enjoy contact sports, as I am still very physically active. I was in a fight about three years ago over money that was owed to me and I ended up in court. The judge described me as 'an extremely violent' woman. I yelled abuse at him from the dock and got another two weeks added to my sentence. I didn't give a damn.

Notices.

Much acclaim for my sermon about the apes who live on the Rock of Gibraltar last week. So many people come up to me and are often awestruck about my endless ability to deliver interesting sermons every single Sunday of the year. Some even presume that I have a team of researchers who help me with my ideas. Nothing could be further from the truth. I'm just naturally brilliant when it comes to the whole 'sermon thing' so drop it.

I have recently lost a book called *Interesting Topics For Speeches – A Bluffer's Guide*. I would be grateful if anyone finding it could return it to the Parochial House.

Ape

OUR PARISH

Craggy Island, April 20, 1997

Is Elvis still alive? This is a question everyone of us has asked at one stage or another, and the answer is usually 'no'. (Except, of course if the question was asked when he was still alive). When looking for the solution to any mystery, the facts have to be looked at very closely. In the case of Elvis Aran Presley, the facts are these – he died in 1977. Against this fact is the theory that he's not dead at all; we've all heard the stories - he's living on Mars; he's running a gift shop in Tuam; he's reincarnated as Daniel O'Donnell. I've always been particularly sceptical about the last hypothesis. One of the basics of reincarnation is that you have to be dead before you can become someone else. But there is little doubt that the lives of Elvis and Daniel O'Donnell overlapped, and they were both walking

O'Donnell

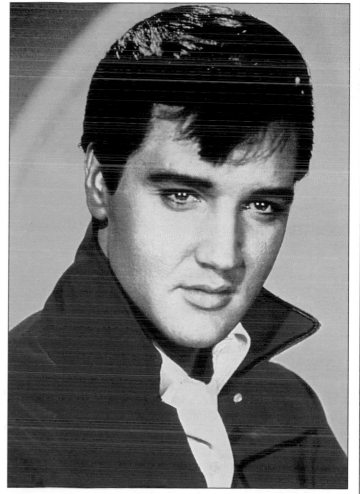

Elvis

around on this Earth at the same time. Thus, I feel personally that the argument for reincarnation in this particular case is a rather flimsy one. And yet I have met a person who believes this scenario, namely Father Eoghan MacDeigan, who, of course, as a Catholic priest, shouldn't believe in reincarnation at all, let alone this frankly mad offshoot of it.

I remember having a debate long into the night in the Kiltiernan Hotel in Malahide with Father MacDeigan about his idea some five years ago, just after he had returned from his theology posting at the University of Santiago. My tactics were simple: I would point out the facts and ask him to argue against them. I presented my case thus: the year is 1976. Daniel O'Donnell is a teenager at school in Donegal. Elvis Presley is still alive. He will not die until the following year. So how can Daniel O'Donnell be the reincarnation of Elvis? Father MacDeigan listened to my argument carefully, taking notes throughout, his eyebrows noticeably furrowing when he thought he saw a weak point in my thesis. When I had finished he went to the bar and brought back two large sherries. I thought I had presented my case well, felt confident of victory, and was looking forward to picking huge holes in his counter argument. However, he soon had me on the ropes. He dragged up all sorts of mumbo jumbo and Latin stuff that I had never heard of, and bamboozled me with mathematical equations. Eventually I agreed with him just so I could go to bed. Daniel O'Donnell was the reincarnation of Elvis after all, I concurred. I had never been so tired in my life.

Moral of the story – Never argue with a theologian.

100 Great Priests

><-+-◇-+-><

5. Father Flip Hendry

Father Flip Hendry was a quiet man. For most of his life as a curate in Ballyderg, Co. Leitrim, where he assisted Father Liam Donegan, he hardly said a word. When he celebrated Mass, he would whisper so low that it was only by paying attention to his hand gestures that his congregation would know what part of the service they were listening to. When not saying Mass, he would sit quietly in the scullery in the parochial house, often twiddling his thumbs, or on most occasions, doing nothing at all.

'He could do literally nothing at all for days on end,' says an old friend of his, Father Cormac Todd. 'He would sit there with a kind of blank expression on his face for most of the day. Sometimes he might think of something

Father Flip Hendry, a quiet type of man

amusing, and he would smile to himself, but he'd never tell you what the joke was.'

However, he did occasionally break out of his shell. Father Todd explains.

'After doing a wedding or funeral he would drink a ferocious amount of sherry and start roaring out the theme tune to *Eastenders* at the top of his voice. He'd go 'Do dee do dee do, dee do, do dee do do, do do do do do do' for ages. He'd always go 'Do dee' as well, never 'Dum dee dum' or anything. He was very particular about that.'

There are many theories to explain the mystery of spontaneous combustion, but none of them can bring back Father Flip Hendry. His parish priest for twenty years, Father Donegan, was the last to see him alive.

'I was eating a ham sandwich in the dining room in the parochial house, and I heard a loud bang from outside. I knew it came from the scullery, where Flip usually was, so I rushed out. When I got to the scullery all I saw was a bit of smoke coming from his shoes and a pile of dust on the floor. I thought I heard a moaning sound coming from the dust, but I can't be sure.'

There was no need to cremate Father Hendry. His unusual demise had already reduced him to dust form. His remains were simply put into an urn and interred in the Church grounds. If he had been asked to comment on his strange death, he probably would have mumbled something softly inaudible, or, more likely, not have said anything at all. But he might just possibly have smiled to himself as he heard the theme to *Eastenders* played from a cassette recorder as he embarked on his journey to the Great Hereafter.

THE HISTORY OF CRAGGY ISLAND
1860-1880

An old-fashioned type engraving. Could this be James O'Connell?

The 1860s were a time of great change on the island. In those years, the first independence movement was formed on Craggy, determined to fight not just for freedom from Britain, but from Ireland as well. James O'Connell was one of the leading figures in this fledgling movement. Having no faith in democracy, O'Connell vowed to use arms to gain independence for the island of his birth, and he formed the island's first revolutionary organisation, 'Craggy Island Revolutions Ltd', in March 1866. However,

intrigue and personal jealousies soon split this rough grouping of poets, schoolteachers and recovering alcoholics, leaving O'Connell and his second in command, Pat Driscoll, as the only true revolutionaries. (The other members left to form a singing group in November.) Driscoll then left the organisation in March 1867 after a row over expenses. However, O'Connell vowed to continue to fight alone. His first plan was to obtain weapons from America, and to this end he organised 'fun

runs' and pub quizzes to raise the necessary cash. Eventually, a small second-hand shotgun was purchased from a gunsmith's in Boston, and O'Connell began his countdown to revolution. He decided that he would seize the local post office and use it as a base for his provisional government, promising free elections within three years. However, when he arrived at the post office, he found that it was closed, so he went home. He then retired from the political scene, writing a memoir and contributing crosswords and brain teasers to Christian Brothers publications.

This wasn't the post office O'Connell tried to seize, and it's usually open anyway

Many legendary stories of sea monsters and strange unusual serpents living off the shore have failed to emerge from Craggy Island over the years, but there is one remarkable tale of a monster which supposedly rented a cottage on the island in the winter of 1870. 'The Cottage Monster' as the creature was known, was believed to have visited the island in the summer of 1868, liked what he saw, and promised himself that he would return shortly. In January of the following year, so the story is told, he approached a local estate agent and enquired about suitable accommodation. When an appropriate cottage was found on the south of the island, the monster moved in. He swam every day, and would occasionally make visits to the local pub, where he drank Guinness and shorts. He rarely got drunk, and was generous when it came to 'getting in his round'. He enjoyed chatting to local girls and said he was from England. Of course, it is hard to separate fact from fiction when it comes to verifying stories like these. Maybe it was a man, not a monster, that rented the cottage on the island. However, many islanders still believe in 'The Cottage Monster', and some local shops sell mugs featuring the fearsome creature.

Danger, monster on the loose

The 1880s saw the arrival of the railway. Tracks were laid at the north of the island, linking a strip of the east coast to the west coast, a distance of seventeen feet. Early

People on 'Penny Farthings'

locomotives were slow, often taking up to an hour to make the journey. While tourists and sightseers could afford to travel at this leisurely pace, for potato pickers and turf cutters it was a major inconvenience, and they were usually late for work, which resulted in stiff fines and floggings being imposed. Often, dissatisfied shepherds would block the line in protest at government cutbacks, delaying the train even further, while bandits were also a constant hazard, holding up the train and playing silly tricks on the passengers. Among these brigands was Pierce McGuckian, a former billiard champion who forsook the green baize for the life of a train robber, and in his later life set up a dental practice with the proceeds of his theft.

Cycling also became popular on the island in the latter part of the nineteenth century. All sorts of contraptions were seen on the island's road, including 'penny farthings' and 'wheel-less' bicycles consisting of an iron bar and a bell that were dragged along the road by their owners.

CRAGGY ISLANDERS ABROAD

A great fondness for Craggy Island has certainly never diminished in the heart of Frank Austin, currently living in **San Jose**. He has recently purchased a large island off the coast of **California** which he intends turning into an exact replica of the isle of his birth. After trimming off the middle section and completely removing the western part, Frank will work from maps and his own memories to create a real-life **Fantasy Craggy Island**. He has also taken out an advertisement in a Hollywood magazine searching for lookalikes who resemble the island's inhabitants and intends to place these at strategic positions. Frank reckons that the whole operation will cost him over **fifty-eight billion dollars**.

Although an **Irish Lesbian Bar** would be a rare sight on Craggy Island, Oonagh Staunton, who emigrated from Craggy in 1990, has recently opened her sixth bar of that type in **New York's Lower East Side**. Lesbianism, a sexual activity where women become 'highly charged' when in the company of other women, became popular in the U.S. in the 1960s, and Oonagh discovered her own latent tendencies when she visited **Manhattan** with friends in the summer of 1988. Although frowned upon in some quarters, lesbianism is now mostly regarded as harmless fun, and an opportunity for women to get together and gossip and interfere with each other away from the prying eyes of men. That's certainly the theme of Oonagh's bars, and they have proved popular with both Irish and American 'lezzers' since the first one opened in 1992.

Craggy Island now has its first celebrity stalker, since the arrest of **Bruce Willis** in Los Angeles last month. Bruce developed a passion for actress **Demi Moore** and spent several months following her around on a bicycle. His activities were ended by the **L.A.P.D.** when he called at Ms Moore's apartment claiming to be her actor husband, who coincidentally has the same name. This may have also led to some confusion on Bruce's part. After a heated argument, the Craggy Islander was arrested and is likely to serve a long sentence in the notorious **Sing Sing correctional institute**.

This is the real Bruce Willis. Craggy Island's Bruce Willis looked nothing like this

JUST FOR FUN!

✱ Note To Parents— Jokes with a slightly 'blue' content have been marked with an asterix.

✱✱ Note to general readers— Jokes with a double asterix indicate that the joke may be recounted here incorrectly, either because a crucial turn of phrase or pun was misheard when the joke was recounted to the editors, or because the joke was recounted incorrectly to the editors in the first place. The editors take no responsibility for jokes that fail to induce the proper response.

Swimming/sinning confusion

(conts: disagreeing with Priest)

A priest was drowning one day and shouted for help. Benjy the lifeguard saw him and dived in to save him. As he finally dragged the exhausted cleric on to the beach, the priest expressed his thanks – 'Oh, you saved my life. Thank you, my son,' he said.

'But Father, you shouldn't be thanking me!' said Benjy with a wicked glint in his eye. 'I've committed a sin!'

'What?' said the priest. 'But you saved a drowning priest – what possible sin could you have committed?'

'Well, Father, let me put it this way ...' Benjy bowed his head and said, 'Bless me, Father, for I have swimmed.'

A Revealing Walk

(conts: Nudity, Priest being shocked/confused)

✱ A priest went to a new parish in County Kerry. He really enjoyed himself for the first week, getting to know his parishioners and going for walks. One day, the weather was really nice and he decided to go for a swim. To his horror, he saw that there were a lot of people on the bench walking around in the nude. He immediately told them to put their clothes on, and they all ran away from him. The next day, he visited a parishioner, and they sat down to enjoy a cup of tea. 'Well, Father,' she said, 'what did you do yesterday?'

'I went for a swim,' he said, 'but I had a bit of an unusual experience. A lot of people on the beach were walking around with no clothes.'

'Oh,' she said, 'you must have gone to the nudist beach!'

The priest was mortified, but when he thought about it, he couldn't help but laugh.

Notice

Due to an assault leading to an arrest at last week's scrabble tournament in the parochial hall, 'Horse Sense' will in future be regarded as two separate words.

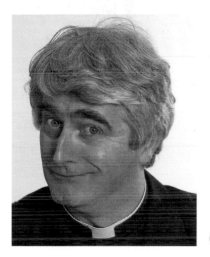

OUR PARISH

Craggy Island, June 29, 1997

'So, Father, was President Kennedy riding all around him or what?'

This was a question which a parishioner asked me after last Sunday's eleven o'clock mass, and I must say it is a question which many people have been asking themselves recently, including myself. It seems that nearly every documentary shown on the television about President Kennedy, and indeed the whole Kennedy family, contains allegations of sexual misconduct. It does indeed seem, that not only 'JFK', but Bobby, Ted, and the whole lot of them were constantly 'at it'. It never occurred to me, as I watched him at New Ross In 1963, that once he went back to America he would be phoning prostitutes and asking them to come back to the Oval Office for a bout of sexual play-acting, probably while Jackie was watching television in the next room. Indeed, recent evidence suggests that if I had visited Marilyn Monroe's beach house in California anytime in the early '60s I would have found the entire Kennedy family (and their in-laws) in Marilyn's bed! And they wouldn't be there to talk about her latest film! No, they'd be there to have sex.

A man who always crops up in these documentaries is Peter Lawford, the Protestant husband of one of the Kennedy girls, a man who was a good actor and who was part of the Frank Sinatra/Sammy Davis Junior 'Bratpack'. It seemed to me that he wore a wig in later years, so I can guess that being deceitful was second nature to him. I only mention him here because a friend of mine, Father Finbar Cudden from Clifden, met him at Boston airport, and asked him for his autograph. He was told to go and 'jump in the sea' or some similarly colourful American expression, and he has been 'persona non grata' with Father Cudden ever since.

Which brings me neatly to the 'Lone Gunman' theory. Who fired that fatal shot from the grassy knoll all those years ago? Was it Lee Harvey Oswald, as many of the experts would have us believe? Or was it Jimmy Hoffa, the hoodlum head of America's Organized Crime Syndicate? Sadly we will never know. The only man who knew the identity of the assassin, President John F. Kennedy, has taken the secret with him to the grave.

What happened next? (!)

33

Jim Sullivan's Sketchbook

Last summer, I was walking along the east side of the island when I came upon Jim Sullivan, who we all know as our retired local government officer, perched on a rock, and drawing a beautiful sunset. I was impressed, and asked him if he had any more examples of his work.

A few days later I found myself in Jim's home, marvelling at folder after folder of the most extraordinary drawings. I thought Jim easily the equal of Monet or someone along those lines. Originally he had taken up art when his wife Elsie had given him a 'painting-by-numbers' kit at the height of that craze in the early 1970s. This is a process where the artist fills in a designated area on a pre-drawn picture in a colour already selected by the Painting By Numbers design team.

Since then, Jim has come a long way, eschewing the 'too constrictive' painting-by-numbers style in favour of a looser, more personal and cohesive vision—a young girl eating ice cream exists comfortably alongside his rendering of a dog startled by its own reflection.

Here's a sample of his work. Look out for more of his art in later editions. I think he's great.

Father McGuire

THE HISTORY OF CRAGGY ISLAND
1880-1900

Although donkeys had always been seen on Craggy, the Great Donkey outbreak of 1880 became one of the most disastrous episodes in the island's history. A particularly randy donkey called Tony had become untethered, and busied himself copulating with many of the local female donkey population. For several months, donkeys were being born at a rate of two a minute until it was reckoned that there were as many as two hundred thousand donkeys roaming the fields and lanes. They were finally rounded up in November of that year, and put into a boat which was moored off Galway.

The Craggy Island Champion became the first newspaper in the history of the island when it was launched in 1886. Although originally just two blank pages tied together with twine, it soon expanded into a two-hundred-page tabloid with a sports section, a lifestyle supplement, and two colour magazines. Although its price tag of two pounds was half a year's wages for the average Craggy Islander, it was a genuinely popular journal, although it's sickening right-wing bias angered many nationalists of the day. It's founding editor was Douglas Weldon, the 'Randolph Hearst' of Craggy Island, who came to the locality in 1880 as a shepherd. After his flock were swept over a cliff in one of the great gales of the time, Weldon went into the newspaper business as an office boy. He was famous for his many pithy phrases such as 'newspapers

Two of Tony's many descendants

Douglas Weldon

are about news, not paper, although the news is actually printed on paper', and 'give the public what it wants, even if you have to queue up overnight in a shop that's selling what the public wants, but is offering it cheap next day because of some kind of sale'. He was deeply unpopular with his employees, often flogging them just for the hell of it, and was notorious for flirting with both male and female members of staff. His reign as editor lasted for nearly fifty years, during the last twelve of which he reeked badly of what smelled like horse manure because of a medical condition.

He died at his desk while dictating a memo on housing conditions in 1933.

Law and order arrived late to Craggy Island in the early 1890s. Before that, there had been little need to enforce penalties for crimes such as theft, because there had been

One of the early uniformed constabulary

nothing on the island worth stealing. Despite the occasional episode of conflict between the Haves and Have Nots, there was also little fighting or violent crime, as the people were so worn out by hunger and disease that they didn't have the energy to hit anybody. However, a rudimentary police force grew out of the popular 'neighbourhood watch' schemes in the 1860s and by the late nineteenth century a local unformed constabulary had become established.

HOUSEHOLD TIPS FOR LADIES, WIVES AND MOTHERS
with MRS DOYLE

3. 'PUTTING CLOTHES OUT ON THE LINE'

HISTORY

Before we talk about preparation, it is worth saying a thing or two about the whole putting clothes out on the line 'thing'. There is a long history of putting clothes out on the line, dating back to Roman times. In those days, Roman ladies would wash their husband's clothes in water without using conditioner, which could lead to a harshness of feel when their husband put their clothes

Some pacifist centurions were known to turn their spears back into washing line poles

on after having come back from the wars. Some ladies believed that by hanging the clothes on the line 'upwind', the creases in their husband's togas and loincloths would curve upwards, decreasing roughness and chafing. However, during the rule of Julius Caesar, the practice died out, as all the poles used for holding the line up were turned into spears in a war against the Gauls, and garments were dried by putting them over rocks and leaving them out in the sun. It was several centuries before clothes were put 'out on the line' again.

PREPARATION

After washing the clothes, put them in a strong metal or straw basket. It is not important for the clothes to be fully dry before they are put up on the line, but 20% to 30% dryness is desirable. Just because the phrase 'don't put all your apples in one basket' applies to apples, doesn't mean that the same thing doesn't go for clothes. If all your clothes fit in one basket, then there is no need to divide up the load into two consignments.

'THE LONG WALK'

If they live in a house with a beautiful garden, ladies can all too easily be distracted by pretty flowers and smells which appeal to their ladylike nature. This is only natural. Ladies like pretty things. But during 'The Long Walk' from washroom to garden, these delights may distract ladies and turn their mind away from the job in hand. Remember: a love of nature will not put the clothes up on the line. Concentrate!

LIFTING THE GARMENTS

Lift garments from the basket one by one, gripping the edges of each garment with firmness and determination. Occasionally, a garment will fall back into the basket accidentally. It is important not to panic if this occurs. It is only a minor setback and there is no need to become embarrassed or ashamed, even if your husband or parish priest sees you. Make a little joke about it; 'butterfingers me!' or 'oh dear' are useful phrases to memorize for occasions like these.

GOOD LINE WORK

It is important to do 'good line work.' Resist the

Blessing the washing as it drys

temptation to become complacent at this stage, just because it is the final part of the procedure. Firstly, clip the clothes pegs on to the empty line, two at a time, approximately three feet apart. Never put the clothes pegs in your mouth as you hang the garment. Lift the garment to the line, drape it over, and unclip the clothes peg on your left-hand side. Attach the peg to the sleeve or shoulder of the garment (depending on personal preference), and make sure that it is held firmly in position. Repeat the procedure with the right-hand side. At this point, the garment should now be firmly secured on the line. (If there are any small dogs in the area, they may try and chew at the hem of the garment, so it is important to banish them to the house or a nearby field.) If you have just attached a heavy item of clothing to the line, such as a bishop's cassock or a scuba-diving outfit, another peg may be added for security. Presuming that your line is facing into the wind, drying should take between three and four hours. Always supervise the drying from a nearby position no further than two yards from the line (you may sit or stand), so that in a sudden gale or hurricane, the clothes may be taken back into shelter.

TAKING THE CLOTHES OFF THE LINE AND GETTING THEM BACK INTO THE HOUSE

After you are certain that the clothes are dry, it is important not to forget to bring them back in the house before you begin the ironing procedure. A dry basket may be used to transport the garments. When lifting the garments check again for dryness, and if you feel any moisture at all, put the item back on the line for another four hours.

When you have successfully transported your 'load', take all the clothes out of the basket and put them somewhere else.

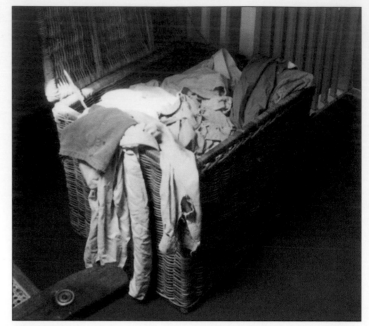
The load

100 Great Priests

6. Father 'Bronco' Dineen

There are many priests who love horse racing. In fact, a 'fondness for the turf' amongst the clergy is as common as their devotion to the odd glass of sherry and the annual holiday abroad to Boston or Rome. However, has there ever been anyone who loved the world of horses more than Father Hal 'Bronco' Dineen?

His route to the priesthood was an unusual one. Raised in Co. Offaly, he left the country in the early '60s to become a manservant to Sheikh Humaf Al Fanim in Riyadh. It was here, in the garden of the Sheikh's royal palace, that he saw his first horse. He noted in his diary, 'It was a brown thing with legs.' Soon, he started riding the beast around the garden at great speed, once knocking down one of the Sheikh's wives as she carried a hot water bottle to the bedroom. For this transgression, he was flogged mercilessly by one of the Sheik's cruel henchmen, Zandor, at that time believed to be one of the most evil people in the world. From that moment on, his days in Riyadh were numbered. He had become disenchanted with the daily grind of palace life anyhow, so in 1969 he left to become a cowboy in America.

He soon joined a rodeo, and learnt all the skills of lassooing runaway cattle that would later be of great benefit to him in the clerical life. When the rope shortages of 1977 left him without a lassoo, he would run alongside cattle, stick his foot out and send them flying in what many thought to be a highly comical manner. For a small man (3' 6"), he was remarkably strong, and in later years he would enthrall his parishioners in Celbridge, Co. Kildare by opening tins of beans with his teeth.

By the mid '70s, as a cowboy recession hit America, he decided to return to Ireland. Seeing Gregory Peck playing a priest on the film in the plane coming over, he was immediately impressed, and applied to the priesthood on arrival at Shannon airport. Four weeks later he was 'in', learning all about God at St Colm's Seminary in Kildare, where he was a contemporary of Father Ginger Aldridge, the famous Yodelling Priest of Loughnane, and Father 'Suggs' McTaggart, who survived for ten weeks in the Himalayas by eating his rosary beads – which luckily for him had been made from dried berries – after a plane crash which killed all the other passengers.

Father Dineen has been parish priest in Tierneybracken, Co. Tipperary since 1980, where the annual rodeo is a highlight of the parishioners' year. He has twice finished as runner-up in the 'Tipperary Person Of The Year' competition.

Notices

Last week's 'Lucky Number' was

5

OUR PARISH

Craggy Island, July 6, 1997

Last Tuesday was a great occasion for everybody here on Craggy Island, as Father Jack Hackett celebrated the fiftieth anniversary of his ordination. This 'Diamond Jubilee' was a marvellous event for both myself and Father McGuire as we joined with Father Hackett in a concelebrated mass to salute this 'grand old man' of the Church. There can be few more respected priests in the country, and it is a testimony to how much regard he is held in in the Irish clerical community that the scuffles which broke out towards the end of the mass ended quickly and without large-scale injuries. The situation was firmly dealt with by the Gardai and they have advised us that in future we should be less generous with complimentary bottles of alcohol. I explained to Sergeant Hodgins that it had been Father Hackett's initiative to get the mass sponsored by Millbush Distillers, and that as a result several priests who took part in the celebration were unfortunately inebriated before the event began. I took full responsibility for the incident and Sergeant Hodgins now considers the incident closed. Sadly, the church authorities have taken a dim view of the sponsored mass initiative, and we have received a rather serious letter from Bishop Brennan on this matter.

Father Hackett has received many letters of congratulation during the last week, and he intends to answer them all personally once his current bout of arthritis has subsided. Five years is probably the timespan we're talking about here.

'A grand old man of the church'

APOLOGY: Bishop Brennan has brought my attention to a phrase I used last week in 'Our Parish', namely 'the post-religious world'. Bishop Brennan is unhappy with a priest of his diocese using this term as he believes it implies that I meant that religion has had its day, and plays no part in the world of the 21st century. Obviously I didn't mean that at all, and think Catholicism is just as valid now as it was a million years ago. Apologies are due to any sensitive parishioners who misconstrued my meaning, either by accident or through feeblemindedness.

THE STORY OF THE CATHOLIC BROTHERS
Part 1

Perhaps no other religious order has had such a profound affect on Irish education as the Catholic Brothers. Providing free education for generations of grateful Irish boys, while at the same time infusing them with a strong religious devotion, has been their mission in Irish life for well over a century. The benefits of a 'Brothers' education are many, and lots of Ireland's public leaders and successful businessmen are proud to have been educated at their many schools throughout the land.

The Brothers were founded in 1802 by Edward Price, a 32-year-old choreographer from Castlebar, Co. Mayo, when he fell off his horse and got a bang on the head. He himself had had none of the benefits of a proper schooling, and often claimed in later life that any knowledge he had was learnt from scraps of paper he found at the side of the road. However, while recovering from concussion after his accident, he became determined to found an organisation that would offer a free education to Ireland's young men.

Although a simpleton with an unusually low IQ living in Penal times, and regarded as 'thick' by even his closest friends, Edward had always had a strong devotion to the Catholic faith, and attended mass up to fifteen times a day, often roaming the countryside in search of secret masses held in ditches and puddles. This inability to ever get enough masses to satisfy his craving led him to consider a career in the priesthood, where he could say as many masses a day as he liked. After discussing the matter in great depth with his parish priest and great friend, Father Hilary Depth, he turned up for an interview at St Colman's Seminary in Swinford in July 1800, hoping to become a 'man of the cloth'. In order to do the written exam, he had learnt English and saved up for a pen, not knowing that St Colman's at the time employed a 'first come, first served' policy; selecting seminarians on the basis of who turned up first, rather than on spiritual and intellectual abilities. Edward had no choice but to return home disappointed. He remained bitter about his experience at the seminary, and in later life would often refer to St Colman's as 'that s***hole'.

For the next ten years, he worked in the family's choreography business, scraping whatever work he could from choreographing light musicals and gay and lesbian dance workshops. But his heart was not in the gay and lesbian dance workshop world, and he longed to devote his life to God. While returning from a shopping spree in June of 1802, his horse, Perfumed Lad, bolted on seeing some explicit sexual graffiti written on the the side of a house, and Edward was thrown from his saddle. He whacked his head firmly off the hard turf, and ended up in hospital. When he awoke, he had an idea that would change Irish society for ever.

Edward Price, founder of the Catholic Brothers, roamed the countryside looking for secret masses.

The fall from a horse that resulted in Irish society changing for ever.

FATHER DOUGAL McGUIRE'S
Holiday Snaps!

India

Paris

Abroad

Hello from Rome

'Back' home

45

Jim Sullivan's Sketchbook

'George Best'

'Girl with an ice cream'

HUGHIE BOYLE ELECTRIC

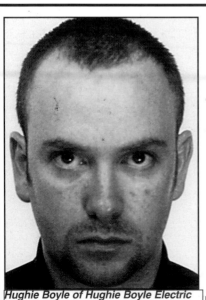

Hughie Boyle of Hughie Boyle Electric

'Hello. I'm Hughie Boyle of Hughie Boyle Electric. People often ask me how we keep prices so low at Hughie Boyle Electric. The answer is simple. Our products are stolen goods that we buy from thieves. We also don't offer a guarantee or back up service on any of our products. You won't find any quality brands at Hughie Boyle Electric, but you will find a large Alsatian in the yard at the back of the shop, so don't get any ideas.

'Come to Hughie Boyle Electric where the bargains are.'

HUGHIE BOYLE ELECTRIC.
GAYNOR'S LANE, CRAGGY ISLAND.
HAVER'S ROAD, CAMBERWELL.

A selection of goods at Hughie Boyle Electric

100 Great Priests

7. Father Barry 'Rasputin' Tarpet

The Church's attitude to female impersonators and what are now known as 'transvestites' has changed little over the years. They have always been seen as deviants, barely better than prostitutes, adulterers, or oral sexers. In the fifth century, it was even sinful to look like a woman (as opposed to looking 'at' a woman, which was also a sin). 'Female looking' men were persecuted under the Treaty of Trieste, and were often chased out of the neighbourhood where they lived by squads of vigilante monks. Michael of Milan, an organic wine grower of the time, writes in his diary about this persecution.

'Was chased today because I look a bit like a woman. 'Tis true I have full lips and a shapely appabellum (arse), but to say that I am a girl is simply daft.'

Father Barry Tarpet lived in more tolerant times, but Kilkenny in the 1920s was still unlike a modern-day Los Angeles or New York. He came to the village of Cairnboro' on the Longford border in 1925, shortly after a spell as a parish priest in Donegal town, where he had earned the nickname 'Rasputin' because of his legendary drinking bouts and raucous behaviour. Though normally a gentle man, he would change under the influence of alcohol, and become, according to one contemporary of

The real Rasputin (not Father Barry!)

his, 'a complete bastard'. He once set fire to the main stand at Listowel racecourse for no other reason than that he wondered what it would look like ablaze.

But Father Tarpet's main vice was dressing up as a girl. 'I can't help it. I just f*****g love doing it,' he told his curate, Father Terry Leaves. He preferred skirts to dresses, and shunned unnecessary ornamentation such as earrings and bracelets. Autumnal shades were preferred to brighter colours, and he despised the other best known cross-dressing priest of the time, Father Pat Withers, for his ostentatious appearance. 'You look like a f*****g peacock,' was his comment when the two men met briefly at the Eucharistic Congress of 1932. That day, in fact, was a momentous occasion for both men. Foolishly, and ignoring all advice, they had decided independently to dress up as women while in the presence of the Papal Nuncio, Doctor Barkanada. Cardinal Slim later approached both men in the hospitality tent and told them that they would have to leave the Church. A fistfight followed, during which the elderly Cardinal lost a front tooth.

Father Tarpet packed his bags (over a hundred of them, full of skirts and blouses) the following month and left for America, where he eventually became a make-up artist in Hollywood, working on such classics as 'Notorious' and 'Arsenic And Old Lace.'

CLASSIFIED ADS

PORTRAIT of a PARISHIONER

Robert Dolan

'My name is Robert Dolan. I collect copies of 'Rumours' by Fleetwood Mac on CD. I now have over six thousand CDs with 'Rumours' on it. Some of these are in mint condition, and are worth a great deal of money, and some are worth even more because of a tiny imperfection. For instance, one copy has the songs from 'Tusk' on the CD, and the cover of 'Tusk'. This raises its value to over thirteen pounds.

My greatest pleasure is sitting in my storage room and going through my collection.

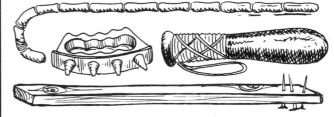
Notices

*'Time has not withered him,
Although the years have turned his face
Into a road map of experience'*

- **Copies of this poem, which I wrote in the style of William 'Butler' Yeats in honour of Father Hackett, are available from the parochial house priced £7.99. The high price is due to photocopying charges. I'm sure, however, that every parishioner will want a copy, and that it could possibly be regarded as sinful not to buy one. (Dictates of conscience in this matter are not allowed.)**

- It has come to my attention that Father McGuire has been handing out rather stiff and unusual penances in confession recently. One parishioner was surprised that instead of an Act of Contrition Father McGuire asked her to go and get him a bag of chips. I have discussed the matter with Father McGuire, and he realises that he has sometimes made mistakes while handing out penances. Priests, like normal people, often make blunders, and a simple misunderstanding can sometimes result in confusion. I have relieved Father McGuire of his confessional duties for the moment, and parishioners should not have any problems of this sort in the future.

OUR PARISH

Craggy Island, October 26, 1997

The All-Priests Holy Roadshow comes to Craggy Island again next week for the second time in six months, and needless to say we're all looking forward to it very much. A death at an entertainment event is always a sorrowful occurrence, but the chances of lightning striking twice are very slim, so hopefully this time around, the night will be remembered for a fun evening out and not a fatal electrocution.

Father Pierce Lally, who proved so popular with our audience last time round, will be 'topping the bill' once again with his popular Sean Connery impressions. Also appearing will be Father Seamus O'Dinn with his popular 'Sounds and Rhythms of Latin America' act involving over a million pounds worth of pyrotechnic wizardry. 'Careful at the front!'

Those of you who liked the hard-hitting satirical stand-up comedy of Father Liam Joyce when he was here in January will be disappointed that he will be unavailable to perform on this occasion. A visual joke about John Major landed him in 'hot water' when he appeared at Jongleurs cabaret club in London recently and he was arrested for gross indecency. Prayers will be said at next Sunday's mass for his speedy release.

Completing the bill will be Father Joe 'Snake Hips' Carroll and Father Swifty Long and His Chorus Girls (court appearances permitting).

Father Swifty Long's Chorus Girls (great fun!)

THE STORY OF THE CATHOLIC BROTHERS
Part 2

When Edward Price left hospital after his horse riding accident in August 1802, he knew that his mission in life would be to found a religious order to educate the young boys of Ireland. With a grant of fifteen pounds from a government 'Start Your Own Business' scheme, he was ready to get his plan off the ground. Wary of other 'holier than thou' religious orders that would ban him from using brutal violence with his pupils, Edward determined to set up on his own, and decided to call his new organisation 'The Catholic Brothers' after a pet dog he had had as a child. Now everything was falling into place. After he ordained himself a Catholic Brother in a ceremony that was subsequently described by someone who had witnessed it as 'little more than a joke', he set up his first school in Ballina in 1803. Initially the school faced fierce opposition from a rival Catholic order, the Oblong Fathers, who ran another Catholic school less than three miles away. But after he paid them a 'sweetener' and promised further donations to their 'building fund' (in reality, a vice ring), the Oblong Fathers decided to leave their rival alone.

Within weeks, Edward was educating boys at a fierce rate; teaching them all kinds of clever things like Latin, Maths, Boxing and tricks with lengths of rope.

By 1822, twenty years after he opened his first school, there were over a hundred Catholic Brothers schools all over Ireland. Famed for their discipline ('kneecapping' – shattering a pupil's knees with a lump hammer, and 'pitchcapping'- forcing a skullcap of hot tar on a pupil's head – were not unknown), the Catholic Brothers soon became the most popular educational establishment of their day, and issued shares on the stock market as early as 1875. Their motto 'Pex Mottinus Eo Et Urp' ('Up And At Em') became a catchphrase in 1889 and was upgraded to a popular saying in 1901. Edward himself died in 1878, a multi-millionaire with houses in Florida, Rome and the Bahamas. His life had been well spent, and although he left the Catholic Brothers three years before his death to become a public relations consultant, we can be sure that he went on to collect his eternal reward in Heaven.

The Catholic Brothers taught the boys to do all sorts of clever tricks with lengths of rope.

HOUSEHOLD TIPS FOR LADIES, WIVES AND MOTHERS
with MRS DOYLE

4. 'CLEANING SHITE OUT OF THE CARPET'

party, and things had obviously got a bit 'out of hand'. As we all know, parties are usually great fun, but there's always someone who 'goes too far' or 'loses the run of himself'. But, of course, the fun stops the next day when the Lady Of The House enters the living room and is greeted by the unsavoury sight of a big lump of shite in the middle of the floor. When I saw my first 'Satan's Coil', it was quite a shock, I can tell you. But I just 'got on with the job' and hoped for the best.

PREPARATION

Firstly, it is important to say, no lady likes cleaning shite out of a carpet. Shite is a horrible word, and a horrible thing, but if you see shite on a carpet, you have to call a spade a spade, and get on with the job.

It is always a shock to see shite lying on the carpet. The thoughts run through your brain – 'How did it get there?' 'I won't like having to clean that shite out of the carpet.' 'I hope no one sees me cleaning that shite out of the carpet.'

PERSONAL EXPERIENCE

My own personal experience of cleaning shite out of a carpet taught me many valuable lessons. It was the day after a wild party at Craggy Island parochial house after Father Crilly's birthday

THE SHOVEL

The first thing to do when greeted with the rather intimidating object, is to use a shovel to remove the 'main body of the work'. This can be then dumped in a bin, or even better, used as fertilizer in the garden. A strong, solid shovel must always be used, as a cheap shovel may break, spilling the shite in the hall or kitchen area.

THE SHAME OF DISCOLORATION

No matter how good a job you do on the shite, the ghostly shadow of its malevolent presence may remain for a long time. It is usually hopeless to claim that it is 'part of the pattern'. Ninety-nine per cent of the time, strangers to the house will know the grim truth. In all likelihood, they will have 'walked that lonely road' themselves. Furniture can sometimes be moved over the offending blotch to hide it, but if the stain is in an awkward spot, the effect can look comical. It is best just to hope that time will eradicate its presence, and to content yourself that you have done a good job under difficult circumstances.

Good shovel.　　*Bad shovel.*

REMOVING THE STAIN

Soap is a lady's greatest ally when removing shite from a carpet. Other carpet cleaners are not really suitable for getting rid of shite, but a good dose of soap and suds usually does the trick. You have to get down on your knees to do a good job, grinding out the shite stain with a wire scrubbing brush or a special 'carpet friendly' brillo pad. Fiddling about with a mop will not get the job done properly, and remember, just because shite looks like chocolate doesn't mean it tastes like chocolate. Don't be tempted, Chocaholic Ladies!

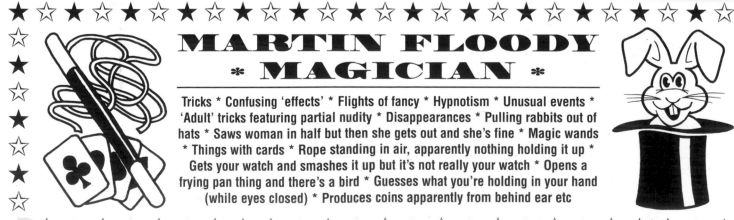

Lives Of The Saints

St Wener

1) ST WENER WAS A SHEPHERD IN SWITZERLAND AND NEVER WANTED ANYTHING MORE THAN A PEACEFUL LIFE TENDING HIS FLOCK.

2) ONE DAY AN ANGEL APPEARED AND TOLD HIM TO BUILD A MONASTERY. HE WAS TERRIFIED AT FIRST, BUT FINALLY SAW THE WISDOM IN THE ANGEL'S WORDS.

4) THE KING OF SWITZERLAND GREW JEALOUS OF ST WENER AND ORDERED HIS SOLDIERS TO ARREST HIM. AN EVIL SOLDIER CALLED OCTOVUS PARTICULARLY HATED ST WENER AND SQUEEZED HIS FEET UNTIL THEY WERE AS THIN AS PLATES.

3) HE BUILT THE MONASTERY IN LESS THAN THREE WEEKS AND SOON BECAME POPULAR WITH SWITZERLAND'S CHILDREN.

5) ST WENER REFUSED TO MOVE THE MONASTERY TO A LOCATION FURTHER AWAY FROM THE KING'S CASTLE, AND WAS CLEVERLY KILLED BY THE SWISS SOLDIERS WITH AN AXE. HE ASCENDED INTO HEAVEN IMMEDIATELY, WHERE HE IS SEATED AT THE RIGHT HAND OF THE LORD, VERY NEAR OUR LADY AND THE REST OF THEM THERE.

A LOOK THROUGH
FATHER JACK HACKETT'S PHOTO ALBUM

'The Connoisseur'. Father Hackett is a lover of fine spirits, wherever they come from.

During the 1950s, Father Hackett spent three happy years in San Pedros, capital city of Panaguray In South America, as chaplain to General Guillermo Paz, head of the military junta. Here he Is seen sharing a happy moment with General Paz overlooking Liberatoras Square shortly after the population had been promised free elections within fifteen years. Father Hackett left the country a matter of hours before the General was hanged from a lemon tree by an angry gang of peasants during a bloody uprising.

Before Father Hackett discovered his vocation, he had many varied careers. Here he Is captaining a ship.

A recent portrait.

Jim Sullivan's Sketchbook

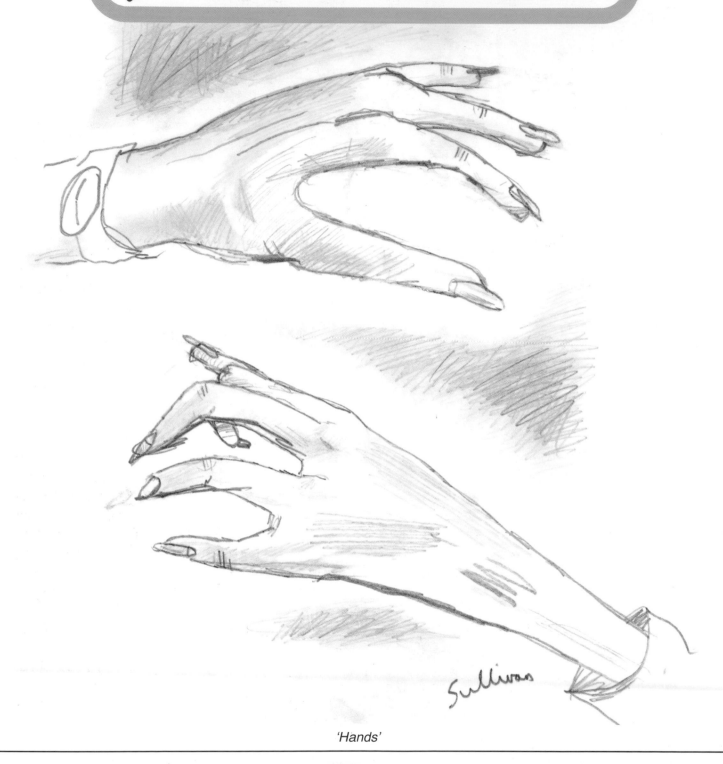

'Hands'

Notices

Several unwanted Easter eggs delivered to the parochial house a couple of months ago are still available priced £6.99 each. There are no discounts for the unemployed.

Thought For The Day

'The devil may have all the good tunes, but if the radio stations don't pay the royalties, then he will be out of pocket.'

OUR PARISH

Craggy Island, January 28, 1998

Last week I spent a large part of my sermon talking about the wonders of modern medicine. I mentioned a story I had read about a man in Australia who was reported to be recovering well after a complicated operation to remove his brain. Always on the look-out for relevant items 'in the news' to give a topical flavour to my little talks, I pounced on this story which I read in the *Evening Herald*, and cleverly slotted it into my sermon on that perennial old theological chestnut: the place of science in the post-religious world. However, in this particular case, I may have acted too impetuously, and should have read the article more carefully. On closer inspection of the report, which was brought to my attention on Monday morning by Father McGuire, I discovered that the Australian man did not have his actual brain removed. It was, in fact, an operation to remove a tumour from his brain. So, not really that newsworthy, except for the fact that this man was an actor and had appeared in over a hundred episodes

A kangaroo like Skippy

of 'Skippy', probably the most famous Australian television show of all time; or at least in the era when they made shows about kangaroos, rather than the type of programmes which are on at the moment, and are mostly set in hospitals. Anyway, my error does render most of what I said in my sermon irrelevant, and for that I apologise if I have caused any confusion or moral doubts amongst you, the parishioners. After all, it's you who pay my wages, and I hope you'll overlook this small error. I'm sure you appreciate the difficulties involved in coming up with a different sermon every week, not to mention this thing you are reading now – my regular popular 'column'. I would also be grateful if you would not mention this little 'gaffe' to people not under my jurisdiction (e.g. other parishes) and especially other members of the clergy. I remember Father Pearse Halliday from Claremorris getting a fierce slagging from other priests at a conference in Lusk a few years ago, after it was revealed that in a sermon he had confused the singer Bob Marley with Hitler. How could he have managed that? we all wondered. But he did.

Anyway, it's never easy thinking up sermons. The rest of the time, one finds oneself on 'automatic pilot', speeding happily through the Offertory and the bit leading up to communion into the shaking hands bit, then 'the home stretch', where I say the thing about the mass is ended, and finally the very last part where I pack up the gear and head to the backstage area (actually my favourite part of the Mass). But for the sermon, your hapless PP is left to his own devices, so I hope an occasional, though very rare, drop in quality can be forgiven. After all, remember, if I forgive you in confession, you can forgive me when we're 'out of the box'.

Lives Of The Saints

1) ST WILFE WAS A COBBLER IN HUNGARY AND NEVER WANTED ANYTHING MORE THAN A PEACEFUL LIFE MAKING AND MENDING SHOES.

2) ONE DAY AN ANGEL APPEARED AND TOLD HIM TO BUILD AN ORPHANAGE. HE WAS TERRIFIED AT FIRST, BUT THEN THOUGHT 'WHY NOT?'

4) THE KING OF HUNGARY GREW JEALOUS OF ST WILFE AND ORDERED HIS SOLDIERS TO ARREST HIM. AN EVIL SOLDIER CALLED LUPUS PARTICULARLY HATED ST. WENER AND STAPLED PLANKS OF WOOD TO HIS HEAD.

3) HE BUILT THE ORPHANAGE IN LESS THAN A MONTH AND SOON BECAME POPULAR WITH HUNGARY'S CHILDREN.

5) ST WILFE REFUSED TO CONVERT HIS ORPHANAGE INTO A DAIRY FARM, AND WAS KILLED BY THE HUNGARIAN SOLDIERS WITH HAMMERS. HE ASCENDED INTO HEAVEN IMMEDIATELY, WHERE HE IS SEATED AT THE LEFT HAND OF THE LORD, VERY NEAR OUR LADY AND THE REST OF THEM THERE.

Jim Sullivan's Sketchbook

Freddie Mercury

Dog startled by its own reflection

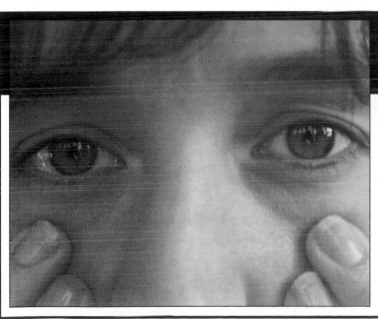

100 Great Priests

8. Father Jimmy Taft

Missionaries hold a very special place in the Catholic Church. The conversion of non-believers to Christianity is a very important duty of the Church, and without missionaries, there would only ever have been one Christian, Christ Himself. (This obviously meant that He had the most difficult missionary job of all time, convincing people that He Himself had come to save the world.)

Library photograph.

Father Jimmy Taft was one of the greatest missionaries who ever lived, and at one stage he claimed to have converted over half the Earth's population to Catholicism. This is an extravagant claim, and there is not much truth in it, but it serves as an example of Father Taft's extraordinary self-confidence and missionary zeal. Having trained at St Patrick's Missionary College in the early 1890s, he left for Africa on July 7th 1896, carrying with him the basic tools he would use to convert the Dark Continent to Christianity: a bible and a big stick. 'Beating' religion into people was a popular method of conversion at the time. 'It is important,' Father Taft told a fellow missionary soon after he arrived in Nigeria, 'that we "knock" religion into these primitive Africans. We can explain the fine points of theology to them afterwards. Don't worry about that now. The main thing is to knock religion into them.' Soon afterwards he set off into the jungle, where he soon cornered some members of the Hembwe tribe. He set about them with his stick, and within minutes had claimed five converts. He told them their first duty as Christians was to inculcate as many of their tribe as was possible into The One True Faith, and with this purpose in mind, he gave each of them a small club and told them to bag a few new believers before tea time. They returned with fifteen each. Father Taft rewarded them with sweets, and then organised a football match.

'The Crocodile', as Father Taft soon became known to the Africans (he had tough, reptile skin that could not be penetrated by either spears or bullets), remained on the continent for the next fifteen years, on average converting fifty natives a day. Sometimes he couldn't stop converting people, with the result that individuals often became Catholics two or three times. When he hit a 'run' like this he wouldn't eat or sleep for weeks, feeding his converting addiction with up to forty locals. He could do whole tribes at a time, and his own personal record was set in Zanzibar in 1999, when he reached a speed of fifteen conversions a second. Inevitably, burn-out occured, and Father Taft suddenly collapsed and died while baptising apes in The Belgian Congo in 1911. He had run out of people to convert, and was submerging a large gibbon in a bucket of water when he suddenly keeled over and fell down a disused mineshaft. A heart attack was suspected, but never confirmed, as his body was never found. Natives believed he had been eaten by giant ants. Little did they know, as they chewed on Father Taft's bones, they were eating one of the great characters of Catholicism.

The sky's the limit!

8. Father Kevin Sparks

'Sparks will fly' was a common joke around St Colm's Seminary in the early years of the 20th century. In those bygone days, men first dreamt of taking to the air and 'flying like the birds', and among these pioneers was a dreamer called Father Kevin Sparks, a young lecturer in the college who hoped that by taking to the skies he would become 'closer to God'. Sceptics, in those times as in the present, were not thin on the ground. 'If God had meant us to fly he would have given us wings' is a common saying today, and it is believed that the phrase was first said by Father Robert Flavan, the senior theological lecturer at St Colm's at the time, during a heated debate with Father Sparks. The mood soon became ugly during their exchange, and several punches were thrown. Early air travel was a 'hot potato' of a topic at the time, with running battles often taking place on the playing fields of St Colm's between enthusiasts and non-enthusiasts.

Father Sparks made his first attempt at flying in October 1901, when he jumped off a small box. Although this was technically 'flying', and he was not unhappy with his initial effort, Father Sparks knew that to go down in history as one of the aviation 'greats' he would have to remain airborne for more than half a second. By carefully studying the laws of physics, he soon began to recognise the crucial difference between flying and merely jumping off a box. His next effort involved leaping in the air from a standing position. This too was modestly successful, and he completed a safe landing after having made a jump of three feet. His next attempt involved flapping his arms wildly at the apex of his jump. As he was hoping against hope that this action would keep him airborne, his inevitable descent was a crushing disappointment to him, and he spent the next few months in a black depression. However, when he got over the failure, the disappointment spurred him on to find other ways of maintaining altitude. In April 1902, he suspended himself under the bridge at Wexford by a rope. Hoping to 'glide like a seagull' when the rope was cut to by an assistant, he merely fell into the river below.

In January 1903, the Wright Brothers made the first successful manned flight in America. Father Sparks realised that they had discovered the secret of aviation that had always eluded him; they used an aeroplane. 'Of course!' he wrote to his cousin, the actress Emma O'Neill. 'It seems obvious now. The Wright brothers have used an engine with a propeller on the end of it. I was merely jumping up and down more in hope than anything else. I think I'll give up this aviation lark now and teach more Latin instead.'

He was true to his word, and ignored air travel for the rest of his life, always preferring to travel by boat when journeying abroad.

GOD'S MARVELLOUS WORKS

No. 109: THE RAINBOW

The rainbow is a gorgeous thing made up of lots of nice colours, and you can usually find it when you look up at the sky (God's Marvellous Works No. 5) after a shower of rain (No. 67). We can tell what are God's favourite colours by the ones He chose for the rainbow: red, yellow, blue etc. He didn't use black because it's a very depressing colour, and also is associated with the Devil, as is red.

No. 110: MOUNTAINS

God created mountains to bring a bit of life to landscapes (No. 56). He may have created them just before he created lakes (No. 78) , knowing that they'd make a nice reflection in the water (No. 2). When people started being born on Earth, they also had a tendency to wander off. God made mountains so they could be hemmed in a bit more, and wouldn't get confused when they found themselves in unfamiliar territory. People who

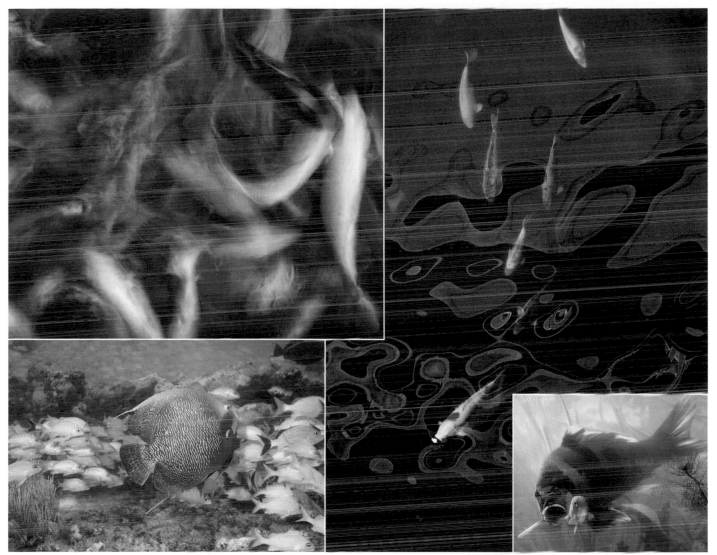

Was God having a laugh when he created these?

live up on the top of mountains, such as shepherds, and especially saints, often feel closer to Heaven (No. 1) and get a tremendous buzz out of it.

NO. 111: FISH

Some fish are so bizarre looking, it looks as though God might just have been having a bit of a laugh! He may have needed a bit of light relief after creating darkness (No. 45) and earthquakes (No. 48). Fish come in all varieties and shapes, but amongst the most familiar brands are trout and mackerel. Unlike animals (No. 5), fish live in the sea. This is one of their most recognisable

characteristics, as well as having fins.

Some of the fish that live in very deep waters are absolutely lunatic looking things. Some of them have antennas! What would a fish want with an antenna, you might ask. Is he trying to tune into RTE?!! No, he's not, of course. It's for something else.

NO. 112: AIR

Without air, we'd all be dead. This is what it means when people talk about 'the gift of life'. The gift is air. God saw that without it, we'd be rolling around on the floor, gasping and shouting for help. But no-one

would come, because there'd be no air anywhere else, and people over there would be shouting and gasping as well. Even people with oxygen masks on wouldn't be able to help, because there'd be no air in the tanks. They'd be rolling around on the floor too, and the people without the masks would be going 'Why are they rolling around the floor as well?' The answer is simple—they have no air.

Air is made up of oxygen and dust. The dust is necessary so that we can see the air. If you're in a room, and the sun (No. 88) is coming through the windows and you can't see any dust in the rays of light, get out quick! There's no air in that room!

OUR PARISH

Craggy Island, April 26, 1998

On Monday, while I was out shopping for a new laser for my CD player (the old one had worn down), a young parishioner named David approached me and said, 'In your sermon yesterday, you said that life was like a ship. What did you mean by that?' I was about to reply when he added, 'Because you weren't very clear.' Then he continued, 'And you kept saying it, even though you never really said why life was like a ship.' I had not even opened my mouth before he added, 'You could have said, "Life is like a football" and it would have made about as much sense.'

Then he said, 'I mean, you come out every week, and you look as if you'd rather be somewhere else, and then you fob us off with some half-thought-out b****cks about life being like a ship. What's that all about? Is that what you get your big house and your housekeeper and your room and board for? Giving us c***p like that? I was half thinking about leaving the church but you made up my mind for me right there. Why don't you take your collar and shove it up your a*se. You're useless. How dare you call yourself a priest. How dare you. No, no, listen to me, "Father" – how dare you. It's people like you ... God, the hypocrisy of it! Not just you, the whole thing. The whole stinking, crumbling edifice. I can't take it any more. I'm going. You'll understand if I don't wish you a good day.'

As he walked off, pausing only to spit on the ground, I thought about what David had said. Was he right? Was I abusing my position and not putting as much thought into my sermons as I should? Then I saw a bird, flying through the sky like an eagle, and I thought, 'We are all like that bird, flying around in the sky. We are all, in some way, like that bird.'

Life is like a ship ...

... and is also like a bird

FATHER BOLAND INVESTIGATES

by Catherine Lysarght

THE COLLECTION MONEY MYSTERY

IT WAS A SAD DAY FOR everybody in Ballaghadrain. New government legislation had forced Sean Fontley, the chemist, to sell contraceptives in his shop, and everyone in the village was in bad form about it. Father Boland was expecting Sean to be concerned when he called in to buy some cough medicine, and sure enough, he was in a terrible state.

'It's a dreadful thing, Father. Me and Mary [Sean's wife of forty years who had problems with her legs] being forced to sell contraceptives.'

'Never mind,' said Father Boland. 'Good Catholics won't buy contraceptives under any circumstances. You have nothing to worry about.'

JUST AS SEAN WAS handing Father Boland his change, Nuala Fleming rushed into the shop. 'Oh, Father,' she exclaimed breathlessly, 'have you heard about Dinny Rush? He was mugged on his way to the post office and all the collection money was stolen!'

Dinny Rush was in charge of the money which was collected at all the masses on Sunday, and always lodged it in the post office on Monday morning.

'That's unfortunate,' said Father Boland. 'I suppose the Guards have been notified.'

'Yes they have, Father.'

'Well, all we can do for the moment is leave it in their hands.

Good day to you both.'

HE LEFT THE SHOP with a lot on his mind. Luckily there was racing from Fairyhouse on the television and Father Staunton had left him a lovely bottle of sherry which he had got in Lourdes. He could put the worries of the parish behind him for the whole afternoon.

THE NEXT SATURDAY, Father Boland was up early to attend the opening of the Ballyneedy Poetry Festival. He didn't have much interest in poetry himself, and much preferred reading detective stories. Like most people, he disliked most modern non-rhyming poems, but there was always plenty of food and drink at the opening of the festival, and he usually had a bit of a laugh when he went along.

He arrived in Ballyneedy in plenty of time for the opening speech by festival chairman Harry Bulfin, and was soon chatting away to many of his friends from the town. One person he didn't recognise, however, was a tall man with a beard who was talking loudly in a group nearby. 'Who is that?' he asked Harry as they both tucked into some tasty cucumber sandwiches. 'That's John Lawrence, one of the modern poets who's just moved to the area recently. He lives in your parish actually, Father.'

'That's funny, Harry. I've never seen him at mass.'

'Really? That's unusual all right.'

'He's a modern poet, you say, Harry. Would I be right in thinking that a lot of his poems don't rhyme?'

'You'd be right enough there, Father. It's very peculiar stuff all right. I don't think he's ever had any of his poems published.'

Father Boland noticed that Mr. Lawrence had been joined by a woman who was laughing heartily at his jokes.

'Harry, is that Mr Lawrence's wife?'

The festival chairman became very hesitant and his mood darkened.

'It's not exactly … his, eh, wife … I think it's his girlfriend. But the terrible thing is, Father … they're supposed to be living together.'

'I've read about that type of thing all right, Harry,' said Father Boland calmly. 'Some people even have children despite the fact that they're not married.'

Harry looked very shocked.

'Well, I've never heard of that

Father Boland knew something was wrong.

Nuala looked shocked

kind of carry-on, Father. But they don't have any children. I know that for a fact. I don't trust them at all, to be honest. She has a very posh accent, and he's a bit cock-sure of himself. Now, Father, would you like another cucumber sandwich?'

'No thanks, Harry. I have to make a quick phone call to the chemist …'

Father Boland dashed off in a great hurry.

Father Boland on the phone

TWO DAYS LATER, Father Boland bumped into Nuala at the butcher's.

'Father, Father, have you heard the news? The Guards have arrested a man for stealing the collection money off Dinny Rush!'

'I'm not surprised at all, Nuala. I can even tell you his name. He's called John Lawrence.'

'Goodness! How do you know that, Father?! I'm very surprised!'

'I simply put two and two together, Nuala. I rang up Sean Fontley on Saturday, and asked him if he'd sold any contraceptives. He said that, yes he had; to a very snooty man with a beard. I knew from this description that he was talking about a modern poet called John Lawrence. Apparently he lives with a woman he's not married to …'

Nuala gasped. Father Boland allowed her a few minutes to calm her nerves and then continued with his story.

'I also learnt that he hasn't had any of his poems published. Another thing I considered was, despite the fact that he is living in a sinful situation with a woman, he has no children. Modern poets are unable to restrain themselves from the sexual act, and are too selfish to have offspring, so they are forced to buy contraceptives.'

'But you said there wasn't any demand for any of his poems, Father. Where did he get the money?'

'From robbing poor old Dinny Rush,' said Father Boland, sadly.

'Well, Father, that's an incredible story,' said Nuala.

'It is indeed, Nuala,' said Father Boland. 'Now if you don't mind, I have to go home for my tea. And then I'm going to finish a good detective story that I've been reading.' And with that, he got up on his bicycle and cycled home to the parochial house for a big feed of spuds.

St Bixen

1) ST BIXEN WAS A PHILOSOPHER IN GERMANY AND NEVER WANTED ANYTHING MORE THAN A PEACEFUL LIFE THINKING ABOUT THINGS AND COMING TO CONCLUSIONS.

2) ONE DAY AN ANGEL APPEARED AND TOLD HIM TO BUILD A HOSPITAL CLOSE TO THE BEACH. HE WAS TERRIFIED AT FIRST, BUT WHEN HIS MOTHER BECAME ILL, HE KNEW THAT THERE WAS NO TIME TO SPARE.

4) THE QUEEN OF GERMANY HEARD STORIES OF ST BIXEN, AND DEMANDED TO SEE HIM. WHEN SHE DID, SHE ORDERED HIM TO STAY IN HER CASTLE AND BE HER WEDDED KING. ST BIXEN REFUSED, SAYING, 'I HAVE NO QUEEN, ONLY A KING. KING JESUS CHRIST.' AN EVIL SOLDIER CALLED HEINRICH PARTICULARLY HATED ST BIXEN AND FORCED A DOG TO BITE HIM.

3) HE BUILT THE HOSPITAL IN TEN YEARS AND SOON BECAME POPULAR WITH GERMANY'S CHILDREN.

5) STILL ST BIXEN REFUSED TO GET MARRIED TO THE QUEEN, AND WAS KILLED BY THE GERMAN SOLDIERS WITH PIKES. HE ASCENDED INTO HEAVEN IMMEDIATELY, WHERE HE IS SEATED AT THE LEFT HAND OF THE LORD, VERY NEAR OUR LADY AND THE REST OF THEM THERE.

GOD'S MARVELLOUS WORKS

No. 113:
AGRICULTURE

Thank heavens for agriculture. If God hadn't made it, dinner time would be very boring indeed!

No. 114: COMPUTERS

One of God's most recent inventions, computers show very clearly the 'modern' side of God. Always to the forefront in the field of technical development, God pulled this one right out of the top drawer and showed that He is just as relevant today as He's always been. Thinking computers up is a tribute both to His ability to keep in touch with modern trends and the excellence of His hard-working design department. Although nobody knows how computers work, very few modern businesses (No. 60) can exist without them. The sheer genius of computers is another example of how brilliant God is. There is no doubt that, as we approach the millennium, the commitment to excellence that we expect from God will continue beyond the year 2000.

THE MIRACULOUS POWER
OF
EGGS

BY EITHNE POWER

In the Catholic Church, eggs are second only to red wine when it comes to miraculous properties. Many diseases have been cured by eggs, including jaundice, leprosy and limbs growing back.

Egg miracles
One of the best known 'egg miracles' concerns the case of Lucy O'Dwyer from Dundalk, who had a great faith in the power of eggs to cure skin discolouration. Lucy came into contact with jazz music in 1933 during a trip to England, and as a result turned bright yellow. Luckily, the power of prayer mixed with the power of eggs was enough to turn her skin back to it's natural off-pink colour. The combination of prayer and eggs have been proved to be a winning formula over the years.

Man brought back to life by prayer and eggs
Everything out of the scope of normal miracles holds no fear for the eggs/prayer combination. Sean O'Boyle from Nairobi (originally from Cork) was brought back to life in 1955 by his sister who furiously prayed and boiled eggs at the side of the road after Sean was involved in a fatal car crash. Despite being dead at the scene of the accident, he was able to walk away from the scene unscathed within minutes.

Eggs and serious sin
Eggs are also great when it comes to forgiveness of sins. A serious sin such a shoplifting can normally be forgiven by reciting a decade of the rosary and ten Hail Marys. However, a few boiled eggs and one Our father can do the job just as well. Eggs have great power when it comes to growing plants in the garden. Tomatoes can grow up to twenty feet in diameter when exposed to the power of prayer and eggs. Also, cucumbers and peas have been known to respond positively.

The future of Eggs and Prayer
Where next for prayer and eggs? Devotion to prayer mixed with apractical belief in the miraculous properties of eggs have been hugely successful in the past, but will the next century be just too full of skepticism and smart alecs to make the propositon of further egg and prayer type shenanigans viable? The answer is, as ever, 'wait and see.'

NEW TITLES FROM

CUCHULAINN PRESS

The Lighter Side of The Famine

T H E LIGHTER SIDE OF T H E FAMINE
C o r m a c   D u n n e

'Just after we left Queenstown, I heard something slip over the side of the boat. It sounded like a very small splash, and I thought a bundle of twigs had fallen into the water. In fact it was Paddy O'Connor from Skibberdeen. At that stage he was down to two stone, and you could see through him when he stood in front of the sun. The whole incident was very funny and we all laughed our heads off. Many fainted ...'

Although four million died in the 'Big Hunger' of the 1840s, there were many funny stories connected with the times. Often hilarious, rarely less than amusing, here is a collection of anecdotes and stories retold by the people who were there and managed to keep a smile on their faces as they stared into the jaws of death.

by Cormac Dunne

Hairy Monsters of Ireland

'It stood before me, growling and making menacing noises. It was unusually hairy, with big teeth, and there was a smell off it like silage. How it had got into the bath I will never know. But I knew then that the legend was true, and that I was face to face with the Big Dog of Nobber.'

HAIRY MONSTERS OF IRELAND

SISTER IMELDA DE BRUN

A collection of blood-curdling tales and chilling stories featuring over two hundred hairy monsters. 'The Hairy Woman of Knock'; 'The Ragged Child of Ennistymon'; 'The Small Man of Rochree' and many more; they're all here in this terrifying volume.

by Sister Imelda de Brun

An A-Z of Ireland's Traitors

A to Z of Ireland's Traitors
Bill Fanning

'Pierce McQuaid was one of the most hated traitors of 18th century Ireland. The government paid him handsomely for his treachery, and his evidence sent nearly half a million brave Irishmen to the gallows. His wicked acts of treason eventually caught up with him and he perished in a marbles attack outside his home in Blackrock.'

Over four thousand of Ireland's most notorious traitors listed in order of infamy with illustrations by the author.

by Bill Fanning

Fairies of Ireland

'Dinny Wall, in old age, recalled an outbreak of fairies in Mayo of the 1890's. "The fairies used to hang out in a field near the graveyard. They were mostly benevolent, except for one bad fairy who swore at the local schoolmistress and mocked her dresssense. The fairies were very white looking, and had wings like you'd see on flies. They were about three inches high and, like flies, if you'd try to swat them with a newspaper, they'd get out of

Fairies of Ireland
Father Jack Larpey

the way really quickly. A lot of them spoke French for some reason, and they were very well-mannered. Once some of the young fellas brought one of them down the pub and tried to get it drunk, but it would have none of it."'

Reflections and memories of fairies in Ireland from 2850 to 1950. Appendix lists fairies in alphabetical order, with full biographies and 'fun' anecdotes.

by Father Jack Larpey

CRAGGY ISLANDERS ABROAD

Seamus Gorton, who left the island in 1976, is now acknowledged as Guatemala's biggest exporter of **crocodile heads**. A fierce man, over 6 feet 7 inches tall, he developed a passion for crocodile wrestling

after a spell in the **Honduran army** in the 1970s, where he acted as a **lookout/sentry/entertainments officer**. After accidentally fatally wounding a **crocodile** in a fight outside a bar, he decided to stuff its head and mount it on a plaque over his bed. It was spotted there by an American crocodile lover, who offered to buy it for fifty dollars, and Seamus was encouraged to go into **crocodile head stuffing** full time. Initially using slave labour, in 1992 he moved operations to a purpose built crocodile head stuffing factory in the heart of the **Guatemalan jungle**, and recently stuffed his fifty thousandth crocodile head, which he presented to **President Mary Robinson** while she was on a recent trip to that troubled Latin American country.

This crocodile's head was eventually stuffed

100 Great Priests

10. Father Joe Salt

Commercialism is very much a part of our modern world. All around we are surrounded by advertising, and every man, woman and child in the country is all too familiar with the cynical 'product placement' antics of Hollywood. In the mid-1980s especially, 'selling' was the word one everybody's lips, and sponsorship and promotional gimmicks were a part of everyone's daily life.

One man who tried to 'sell' the Church to likely 'customers' in this way was Father Joe Salt, parish priest of Kilmacduggan in Waterford from 1983 to 1988. Very much influenced by Peter York and the successful methods employed by the Saatchi and Saatchi advertising agency in London, Father Salt realised that if the Church

Father Joe Salt working on a new scheme

was going to survive in a competitive market, and fight off the counter-attractions of bingo and drug abuse, then an 'eighties' outlook was definitely needed.

First off, he decided to get the Friday evening confessions sponsored by a local double glazing firm. This 'Callahan Bros. Double Glazing' Confessions, including promotional gifts and free estimates, proved hugely popular, with over a million sins being absolved in the first week alone. Spurred on by the success of this venture, Father Salt's next enterprise was a First Communion sponsorship by 'Kenny's Hardware'. Individual weddings and funerals were then sponsored by various local businesses. During burials, banners such as 'Today's Funeral Generously Sponsored By Dundalk Tyres' were a common sight, and on occasion the coffin and candles used in the ceremony were also individually donated in return for publicity for the manufacturers.

PORTRAIT of a PARISHIONER

Denny Paine

My name is Denny Paine. I have terrible sunburn, and no-one likes to sit beside me on the bus. It's not my fault! My father gets it too. My sunburn is so bad it spreads onto chairs and the carpet. Once some of it spread onto the cooker and got into the food. Despite all that, I have had great success with 'the ladies' because of my fantastic personality and the fact that I was on a television quiz show a few years ago. The effect of the studio lights on my sunburn caused my skin to turn more blazing bright red, and no amount of make-up could stop me from looking like a big tomato. Friends of mine who saw the programme had to turn down the colour on the televisions.

I finished fifth in the quiz.

Soon, however, many parishioners began to become less enthusiastic at what they began to see as 'over commercialisation'. One wedding in particular proved controversial when the company sponsoring the event, 'Hilary's Beauty Shop', complained that the bride was not attractive enough, and that the image of their shop could be harmed as a result of the association. Their request for a last-minute replacement bride was turned down by her family, despite desperate pleas from Father Salt.

However, this commercialism was perhaps too 'eighties' to last. Manufacturers and firms gradually turned away from Father Salt's propositions to sponsor his various activities, turning their attentions instead to more glamorous events such as water-skiing and rock band competitions.

Disillusioned with the clerical life, Father Salt turned professional at clay-pigeon shooting in 1990, and he currently lives in Canada.

Jim Sullivan's Sketchbook

Father Hackett

ART COMPETITION

The winner of our recent Parish art competition is Mrs D. Coogan of Scilly Road. The standard was high among all four entries, but this charming ensemble portrait entitled *We Can Work It Out* wins the coveted first prize of £2 worth of lottery tickets

IF YOU LIKE HISTORY AND EGGS, THERE'S ONLY ONE PLACE TO BE

History is part of all our lives. It's happening all around us. It's in the food that we drink and the air that we breathe. It's in the bones of small children and the hair of beautiful young girls. It's up trees and in valleys and cars. It's in the morning air and the stench of death at night. It's all over the place. Eggs are also part of our lives as well.

Come and visit the **CRAGGY ISLAND MUSEUM OF HISTORY** incorporating **THE EGG ZOO**,
The Harbour, Craggy Island
(Please note; Egg part of museum does not include historical eggs.)
OPEN MONDAY TO SATURDAY, 10 TILL 5.

Pregnant women please note; exposure to some types of egg on display may lead to complications during later stages of pregnancy

---

Words of Wisdom

'One must never give up a fight, especially if one is a professional boxer.'
Muhammad Ali

OUR PARISH

Craggy Island, June 7, 1998

I'd like to try and put a stop, once and for all, to a scurrilous rumour that has been circulating around the parish.

A little while back, there was an advertisement on British television for a volunteer police force. The ad showed an actor, standing on a bridge, pretending he was about to jump off. Some people came up and tried to stop him, and I suppose the point was that these people are the type they want for the force.

Now, I have heard it said by more than one person that I myself – Father Ted Crilly – am clearly visible in the advertisement giving the man a 'wide berth'. Nothing could be further from the truth. If it is me in the advertisement (I did visit London a few years ago, so I suppose there's a slight chance it might be), I'm sure I didn't approach the man, for a very good reason. I may have been afraid that the man was not a practising Catholic, and that the sight of a priest in full 'combat gear' may have enraged him to such an extent that he would have jumped off out of sheer spite. If I had known the man was an actor, and there was a camera crew present, I would not have hesitated one second in speaking to him.

I find this whispered talk of 'scaredy cat' and so on quite unbearable. I am not a scaredy cat. Recently, I saw an old woman being threatened by two toughs and, without any thought as to my own safety, I rushed to a phone box and called the police. While waiting for them to arrive, I kept an eye on the two toughs and made sure they didn't run away. When the woman had handed over all her money, the toughs tried to make their escape. Again, I did not pause. I ran back to the phone box and insisted that the police hurry up. They were there within minutes. Are these the actions of a 'scaredy cat'? I think you all know the answer to that.

A bridge

FATHER BOLAND INVESTIGATES

by Catherine Lysarght

THE MYSTERY OF THE RUDE LETTER

Father Boland had noticed something unusual in the sacristy that morning. Along with his neatly laid out vestments and the usual paraphernalia for saying mass, was a crude scrawled message on a piece of paper which stated simply: 'I'm going to get you, Father Boland, you little c**t.' What could this mean? He had no enemies in the parish, and the only person he could think of who held a grudge against him, Jimmy Henderson, was inside jail in Dublin, serving fifteen years for buggery.

After a hearty lunch served by Mrs Cullen, he settled down to watch the Prix De L'Arc De Triomphe on television. He had a bet on 'Fancy Dan', and was delighted when the nag romped home fifteen lengths ahead of the rest of the field.

The next morning, Father Boland went to collect his winnings in the betting shop. As he entered, an arrogant man with a posh accent brushed past him. 'Out of the way, there! I have to go to church!' 'What a rude man,' Father Boland thought to himself.

Mrs Phelan seemed slightly out of sorts as she handed over the five pounds. This surprised Father

Boland. He thought she would have been happy, as she had just come back from Lourdes, where she had received a miracle cure.

'What's wrong with you, Mrs Whelan?' asked the cleric. 'I hope it's not because I've cleaned out the betting shop!' 'No, Father,' she replied. 'It's because someone put a piece of paper with a message on it through my letter box, and I'm afraid I'm a bit upset about it.'

'That's very strange,' said Father Boland. 'Someone has sent me an unusual note as well. Would you mind if I had a look at your note?' 'No, Father,' said Mrs Phelan, 'although the language used in it is a bit strong. I'll get it from upstairs.'

A few minutes later, Mrs Phelan returned with the note. On it was written: 'Mrs Phelan, you've got a head like a f***ing turnip, and your husband's p***k is septic.'

'This is most unusual,' said Father Boland. 'What should we do?' asked Mrs Phelan. 'Should we report it to the Guards?' 'Leave it with me for the moment,' replied Father Boland. 'There's no point in troubling the Guards with a minor matter like this. Let's wait a while and see if this fellow gets up to more of his tricks.'

The next day Father Boland was walking along the beach when a ball bounced across his path. He heard a voice behind him: 'Kick the ball back, you dirty bast... Oh, it's you, Father.' The cleric turned around to see young Timmy Collins and a

few of his school friends. 'I'm sorry, Father,' said Timmy, 'I didn't know it was you. Could you kick the ball back please?' 'Yes, of course,' said Father Boland. Then he had a brainwave. 'Timmy,' he said, 'I wonder if I could have a sample of your handwriting, please. We're having a "lovely handwriting" competition in the parish, and I think you might have a chance of winning.' 'Oh, I don't know, Father,' Timmy said. 'I have to go home for my tea now... I'm a bit late.' With that, he kicked the ball in the opposite direction and ran after it.

The next day, Father Boland went down to the betting shop again. Mrs Phelan was anxious to find out if his investigations had led him any nearer to finding the culprit. To

her delight, he was able to say that he was almost certain he knew who had sent them the dirty notes. 'Who is it, Father?' she asked excitedly.

'Who was that posh man who was in the betting shop the other day?' asked Father Boland.

'That's Mr Hetherington-Smythe,' explained Mrs Phelan. 'I don't like him very much. He's moved here recently, and has a lot of airs and graces about him.'

'Mrs Phelan,' said Father Boland, gravely. 'At first I thought young Timmy Collins might be the culprit. He often uses very rough language. But I remembered that his spelling isn't very good, and that he's a bit embarrassed about it. Sure enough, when I met him the other day and I asked him for an example of his handwriting, he

Mrs Phelan seemed slightly out of sorts

Father Boland always enjoyed a cup of tea after solving a mystery.

ran away.'

'Mmmmm,' sighed Mrs Phelan, rubbing her chin. 'Who could the culprit be then?'

'It's Mr Hetherington-Smythe,' said Father Boland.

'No!' gasped Mrs. Phelan. 'How can it be?'

'Well,' said Father Boland, 'he's very posh, and he has a lot of airs and graces about him. I also noticed that the other day he said

he was going to "church", rather than "mass". That can only mean one thing: he's a Protestant.'

Mrs Phelan gasped again. 'But why would he send us dirty notes?' she asked.

'He probably has some grudge against Catholics. Maybe he's just jealous. But he singled us out because I'm the parish priest, and you because you've just received a miracle cure at Lourdes.'

'Well, Father,' said Mrs. Phelan, 'I don't know how you do it. I certainly won't be taking any bets from Mr Hetherington-Smythe again. He seems like a real tool. Anyway, would you like to come inside for a cup of tea?'

'Yes, please!' said Father Boland, smiling. He always enjoyed a cup of tea after solving another mystery.

GOD'S MARVELLOUS WORKS

NO. 115: SPACE (I)

Space ... the final frontier. So said Captain Kirk in his captain's log, all those years ago in the future, and indeed, Space is the one place in the world which, despite attempts to 'tame' it by scientists such as Stephen Hawking, continues to be totally unknown apart from the bits near Earth (No. 12).

Poor old Stephen Hawking. As if the whole of Space could be explained in one book! But we must not laugh at scientists who think they know all the answers. In their own naive way, they are searching for the truth too. If only they stopped looking out at the stars, and into their hearts, they might find it.

NO. 116: SPACE (II)

Not to be confused with Space (I) (115), this kind of space is the kind that we find around us in the countryside, in parks and in the boot of large estate-type cars. This space is even more mysterious than the space it shouldn't be confused with, as it seems to be air (no. 112), but it's even more useful! Not only can you breathe it, but you can also use it to put things in (boxes for stereo equipment etc), and to move around in.

To make it as clear as possible: when you see a thing, pick it up and put it somewhere else. Now, look at the place where that thing that was and imagine the thing you moved back in the same place. Think

of the shape of it. Now, inside that shape is space. You're literally looking at space! Amazing.

Not much space at all

Father Crilly

100 Great Priests

11. Father Buggles Smythe

Nobody ever heard a bad word against Father Leo 'Buggles' Smythe. He was one of the nicest priests ever to 'wear the collar', and his sunny disposition could brighten the darkest hour. He never took Catholicism too seriously, and at the end of the day admitted that there probably wasn't that much difference between all the religions in the world. He had a childlike air about him; so much so that he still retained his baby teeth well into his forties, and always remained bald. People who first met him when he was in his twenties would often remark on his premature hair loss, but his response was always the same: 'Sure I never had any in the first place!' He also liked to sleep in a large cot with bars on it. 'I never grew up,' he told an interviewer on Cavan local radio once. 'Maybe that's part of the problem,' he added ominously.

He would often be seen kicking a ball up against the gable end of his parish church at Rabbitstown on long summer evenings, and loved playing marbles with the baby infants in the yard at Kiltubber national school. His best friend, he once claimed, was a five-year-old named Michael Finley, and he would often arrive at Michael's house in nearby Mullintullet with enough Lucky Bags to keep the two of them amused for the entire evening. Today, that type of behaviour might be regarded as suspicious, but Father Buggles would have been as incapable of having an impure thought as he would be of missing an episode of *The Magic Roundabout*. He also enjoyed dancing and played a mean game of charades. (During an evening with the Bishop of Ferns, his masterly gesticulation to demonstrate *The Effect of Gamma Rays On Man In The Moon Marigolds* was so precise that His Grace guessed the film within three seconds.)

His massive nervous breakdown, when it came, was as spectacular as it was unexpected. He revealed to his stunned parishioners during a St Patrick's Day sermon that he believed that he was a gnome. 'I'm some type of gnome,' he explained. 'I might be an elf as well. But there's definitely some kind of gnome/elf thing going on.' His recovery was long and painful. He never returned to Rabbitstown, but took up an offer to work on the missions in Africa. He can briefly be seen as an extra in Dino De Laurentis' 1976 remake of *King Kong*, but little has been heard from him since. All who remember him hope he is still hale and hearty.

Father Buggles Smythe can be seen in this photo from the 1976 remake of **King Kong**

CRAGGY ISLANDERS ABROAD

The uncanny connection Craggy Island has with the Miss World competition continues to amaze. No less than sixteen contestants at this year's tournament in Thailand have ties to Craggy. Miss Sri Lanka, nineteen year old **Ruindi**

Shik, is a native of the island, and worked for a short time after school in the rope factory on the island's south side. The Iranian entry, **Alasa Hussein**, has a maternal grandmother, **Mags O' Connell**, who hails from Craggy, and Miss South Vietnam, **Tik Tapo**, has an uncle living in a cave on the island's south side. Other contestants who can claim a link to the island are Miss Angola, Miss

Beauty queens. Aren't they lovely?

Siam, Miss Shangri La, Miss Bosnia, and Miss Former Yugoslav Republic of Macedonia.

Terry Nelson is doing very well for himself as a jockey in Indonesia, we are told by his aunt, **Myra Hollins**, who celebrated her seventy-fifth birthday recently; the first time she's reached the dreaded three-quarters of a century mark. After  studying to become a jockey at the Curragh School of Jockeying in Kildare, Terry moved to Hong Kong in 1988, where he became attached to the Hing Ping Stable. Myra tells us that since his move to Indonesia in 1993, Terry has had to get used to a very different type of jockey career. Instead of horses, the tradition in Indonesia is to ride giant pigs around a circular track until the jaded animal is driven to exhaustion and eventual death, while being submitted to the blood-curdling screams and taunts of frenzied locals.

 The last jockey on a live pig is deemed the winner, and although the financial rewards are minimal, the triumphant jockey is usually brought for a drink in a local bar. Terry has become a bit of a celebrity due to his success, having much the same status in Indonesia that Gary Lineker had in Japan when he was playing with Grampus 8.

CRAGGY ISLANDERS ABROAD

Mrs Eileen Long, a native of Craggy Island since her birth in the late 1940s, got more than she bargained for recently when she complained about the colourful language used by a bellboy at the Regency Hotel in Nassau, the capital of the Bahamas.

Unfortunately for Eileen, the bellboy (whom she alleges she overheard referring to her as a fat a**e as she attempted to hire a taxi in reception) is apparently the nephew of a witchdoctor on the island. Reacting vengefully to her complaint, the boy asked his uncle to put a spell on Eileen, invoking the deadly brand of local voodoo known as Obeah. As a result of this evil curse, Eileen has taken on many of the characteristics more often associated with trees, growing a strange bark around her body and growing branches and leaves out of her head. A visit to another of the island's witchdoctors failed to secure an antidote, and

Eileen may have to become accustomed to her new condition. She is hopeful of shedding some leaves in the autumn and local doctors have ruled out the possibility that she may be turning into a rubber plant.

Words of Wisdom

The meek shall inherit the earth and inheritance tax shall test their meekness

An Open Letter to the readership

Dear 'Our Parish' readers,

For years, I have been using 'Our Parish' as a way of getting word of my plumbing business across to all of Craggy Island's inhabitants. Father Crilly's predecessor, Father Benjy Carr, never asked for payment for the service as he felt it would be immoral to accept money for what he considered a pleasure – namely, doing a favour for a friend trying to start a small business.

However, as soon as Father Crilly took over, he imposed a ludicrously high rate for advertising space. This makes it impossible for me to continue advertising my services in 'Our Parish'.

I believe that Father Crilly, behind the public facade, is in reality a cheap, greedy little man. He wants money, and nothing beyond that is important. Not community, nor religion, nor friendship. In order to prove this, I have decided to pay for the space to write this letter, absolutely sure that his love of money will override any feelings of embarrassment, and he will print it in full.

The space for this letter costs £85. Father Crilly is a prick. You see?

Yours sincerely,

Desmond Boyne

Lives Of The Saints

 St Hondo

1) ST HONDO WAS AN ACROBAT IN POLAND AND NEVER WANTED ANYTHING MORE THAN A CAREFREE LIFE ON THE HIGH WIRE, ENTERTAINING HIS CIRCUS FRIENDS.

2) ONE DAY AN ANGEL APPEARED AND TOLD HIM TO BUILD AN ACTIVITY CENTRE NEAR LODZ. HE WAS TERRIFIED AT FIRST, BUT THEN WENT ALONG WITH IT.

4) THE LORD PRO-TECTOR OF POLAND HEARD STORIES OF ST HONDO, AND DROPPED DOWN FOR A GAME OF DARTS. WHEN ST HONDO CLOSED THE BAR DOWN AT ELEVEN, THE LORD PROTECTOR BECAME ANGRY THAT HE COULDN'T GET ANOTHER DRINK. HE SET HIS SOLDIERS ON HIM, AND ST HONDO WAS ROUGHED UP BY A LARGE THUG CALLED WIEDIZC, WHO USED A TWIG TO WEDGE HIS MOUTH OPEN WHILE HE POURED NEAT VODKA DOWN IT.

3) HE BUILT THE ACTIVITY CENTRE IN A FEW DAYS AND SOON BECAME POPULAR WITH POLAND'S CHILDREN.

5) HE ASCENDED INTO HEAVEN IMMEDIATELY, WHERE HE IS SEATED AT THE LEFT HAND OF THE LORD, VERY NEAR OUR LADY AND THE REST OF THEM THERE.

John & Mary's Shop.

'A Legend on Craggy Island since before records began'

Spanners, sweets, cat food, pinking shears, toilets, armbands, luxury items, 'tools of the trade', oven chips, discreet escort agency, publishing house.

New Video Department Opening June 27th featuring special Keanu Reeves section.

Opening Ceremony performed by John McMenamin, fresh from the Moate 'Stars In Their Eyes' competition where he finished third as

Keanu Reeves

Do not miss this once in a lifetime to meet someone who looks like

One of Hollywood's greatest stars